Favorite Recipes

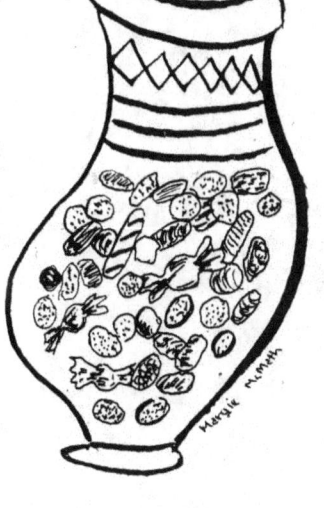

From

Brookside School Cranbrook
REVISED EDITION

Family-style meals, good nutrition, and student and faculty conversations have been important mainstays of Brookside lunches. Some of those special recipes which have delighted children for 85 years are reprinted in this book.

We hope that your favorite dining hall memories will be rekindled with the many "tastings" from Brookside past.

Follow the bees!

Arlyce M. Seibert
Director of Schools

The Publisher wishes to gratefully acknowledge the kind assistance
of the following individuals and offices in the publishing of this book -

Elizabeth C. Clark, Jock and Sue Denio, Wallace and Mable Cripps,
Harold and Jean Smart, Carolyn Tower, Constance Heidt,
Janet Hawksley, Susan Rice, Joan Page O'Hara, Donald Brown,
Gloria Lusk, Douglas Cooper, John Leslie, Liz Lent, Arlyce Seibert,
Mark Coir and the Cranbrook Archives

Copyright © 2022 by McNae, Marlin and MacKenzie Publishers, Ltd.
and the Cranbrook Educational Community. All Rights Reserved.
Printed in the United States of America.
Except as permitted under the United States Copyright Act
of 1976, no part of this publication may be reproduced,
stored in a retrieval system, or transmitted, in any form
or by any means, electronic, mechanical, photocopying,
recording, or otherwiese, without the prior writtem
permission of the publisher.

ISBN 13: 978-1-64136-165-1
ISBN 10: 1-64136-165-4

Library Of Congress Control Number: 2007928645

Illustrations - By Students of Brookside School selected by
Harold Smart
Cover Photographs - John P. Denio
Back Cover Photos of FLora Leslie - Courtesy, John Leslie

Brookside Faculty Members
Remember Flora Leslie

I can't tell you how much I admired Flora Leslie and her magic with food. She was an important cog in the education of the children here. She believed children should be exposed to new foods, since they aren't generally creative with what they eat. You know, they tend to like peanut butter and jelly and that sort of thing.

I remember she used to make cabbage, just plain cabbage, and everyone loved it. She worked to make lunchtime a learning experience just as much as English or math, going around the lunchroom getting the kids to try things.

If one of the teachers was sick they'd go to her and she'd help get them through the day. I can remember a time or two when I needed her help.

The students used to complain that the food at school tasted better than the food at home. And if one of our students continued onto Kingswood they all complained that the lunches weren't nearly as good.

I can't describe our 6th grade dinners in the dining room where I played my ukulele in the bucket Brigade.

About my first lunch at the school, the 1st day of school; I remember looking around the dining room at the teachers' places and noting that I was the only one with a salad. After lunch I took Flora aside and quietly told her privately that I shouldn't have a salad unless all of the faculty did, as this was evidence of a double standard of treatment that I didn't want the children to see.

I know she was doing this as she must have always done for Miss Winter, but that this as a good time to stop doing it. She was initially disturbed, but I assured her I was very pleased with the great meal and the salad, and gently explained to her why it was not a good idea. She was gracious and said something to the effect that she understood my reasoning and had no difficulty with not doing it in the future. And we had a wonderful, cordial relationship from then on and eventually she offered salads staff occasionally.

Jock Denio

Flora was the epitome of graciousness as well as being a fantastic dietitian. I don't believe that any Brooksider of her time could forget the sumptuous array of cookies that she could create for special occasions. She catered for many Brookside events as well as for the Headmistress and families who requested her services. Often her loyal staff went with her whatever the occasion.

Her husband George succumbed to cancer at age 39. Stoically, as best she could, she did not let her worries and cares become another's burden. She continued to stay on at Brookside until she herself reached the age of retirement.

Wallace and Mable Cripps

Memories Of 42 Years At Brookside.

How does one begin to sift through memories of teaching art forty-two years at Brookside? I think fondly of the special times when children sketched by the Brook or from the Tower and the excitement of opening the kiln to see the wonderful animals with their bright glazes, created by "young sculptors", emerging, to the delight of all. I still remember the struggle of students to complete, successfully, acrylic portraits which would be hung proudly in the halls around the Library. I remember the delight in the eyes of the sixth grade students as they polished their newly soldered, sterling silver rings and bracelets or finished acrylic pendants and letter openers. Special were the times we were able to display the student artwork in the galleries of the Art Academy and host an opening for parents to view the special work done by their children.

When I think of the Dining Room, I think of children climbing scaffolding to paint the mural with their renderings of folk characters that were in the songs, sung after lunch. What a wonderful way to end the special "Mrs. Leslie" meal that singing was. The mural, unfortunately, has long since disappeared. The children certainly enjoyed the challenge of doing illustrations for this cookbook with its special Mrs. Leslie recipes.

Special also was the challenge to write, direct, and stage the "holiday" play for 30 years with the wonderful collaboration of Carolyn Tower and Connie Heidt doing the always exceptional, inspiring music with Betsy Clark's lyrics. Recently I was reminded by a current faculty member how she, as a 5th grade student, enjoyed skating with me on Kingswood Lake during sports period at the end of the school day.

One cannot count the number of "special students" all creative in their own unique ways, who made my years at Brookside such a pleasure. How fortunate I was to be in such a unique setting.

And finally, to be asked to chair the Art Departments of Cranbrook, Kingswood and Brookside, as the schools became "one school". My ten years in that position surely was the highlight of my career at Brookside. Memories do linger to be recalled with great pleasure!

Harold Smart

My Experiences in the Dining Room

Soon after I began my forty years at Brookside as the school nurse, I was asked to write a curriculum and teach classes to each grade involving excellent health habits. Good nutrition was stressed in Kindergarten and First Grade as the children began eating in the Dining room. When the salad bar was introduced to the Dining room I encouraged them to try a few raw vegetables. Every day one of the First grade boys, named Johnny, returned from the salad bar with only a circle of croutons and Ranch dressing as a "dip". If I suggested even one vegetable, he would smile sweetly and say, "This is my favorite". Early in January that year I had a skiing accident resulting in a leg cast which confined me to my office. One day Johnny was the student sent to ask me what I would like for lunch? Without thinking I said "Surprise me"! Later he arrived, smiling, and handed me a plate of croutons and dip saying, "It's my favorite".

This story has a happy ending. In May Johnny was again assigned to my table. The first day he proudly returned from the salad bar, eyes dancing, as he showed me three raw vegetables—and it went on from there.

Jean Smart

Flora Leslie! I'll never forget her smiling face, her familiar Scottish burr, her incredible kindness, and, of course, her insistence that the food she prepared and served to her students should be wholesome and "made from scratch": true mashed potatoes, real biscuits---and wonder of wonders---fresh broccoli that retained its proper flavor, bright color, and encouraging crunch. Who knows how many Brookside girls and boys learned to enjoy a wider variety of vegetables after hesitantly tasting that first English pea or slice of carrot or kernel of corn? We were all fortunate recipients of Flora's respect for good food and her devotion to its exceptional preparation.

Betsy Clark

Leafing through the "Favorite Recipes from Brookside School Cranbrook" brings to mind Marcel Proust's famous book; "Swann's Way". The story illustrates the importance of the senses of Smell and taste in bringing forth a stream of consciousness-----sudden and complete remembrances of things and times past. Whenever I taste what is now in today's world referred to as a "rice crispy treat", I think of Flora Leslie's wonderful contribution to the Brookside dining experience in the 60's and 70's. Among my favorite memories of her years as "chef extraordinaire", were the special small and elegant salads in the teacher's place at each table. Another was the singing of the "Johnny Appleseed" grace before sitting down to lunch.

I have tried to choose my "top ten" list of recipes, all of which —like Proust's madeleine, inspire the taste buds to begin working: The Ruby Salad (grapefruit sections and green grapes in a strawberry jello mold); Frankfurter Casserole; Potato Chip Casserole; Ham Loaf: Salmon Loaf; Sherwood Hot Dogs; Pizza (Brookside Style); Brownies; Chocolate Rice Crispy Bar; Apple Salad. Out of the ten, eight were Flora Leslie's personal recipes. She was truly a unique, unforgettable and very great Scottish lady!

Carolyn Tower

Flora Leslie...the consummate lady! This kind, gentle and soft spoken woman was respected by all in her acquaintance; students faculty, parents and staff. She was a dear person! The dining room at Brookside was rare when compared to other elementary school lunchrooms. Not only were the tables set to perfection, but the food was invariably delicious, from side salad, to entrée to dessert. The white fish, often served on Fridays, was equal to any fine restaurant! The entire lunch experience was a pleasant and special part of the school day, with one always looking forward to sharing it with others. This was directly attributable to the skilled and accomplished woman in charge, Flora Leslie.

Connie Heidt

Flora Leslie's food was not only delicious, but very well balanced, healthy and nutritious!

Janet Hawksley

It's been 35 years since I passed through the portals of Brookside School Cranbrook, so, with a nod to Jock Denio, I want to orient myself at the start. I walk through the door and wave at Jock's and Mable Cripps's offices on the left, but turn right down the hall. On my right I pass the hallway to Janet Hawksley's room and the library, continue past the room used by J. Page and Doug Cooper on the left, then move past my own headquarters next to the room where Vicki Gloor and then Betsy Clark taught 6th grade homeroom and Wally Cripps taught math. I pass Mr. Gerhardt's room and go down the stairs to the dining hall. This was Flora Leslie's domain, home of good aromas and better tastes.

I take a seat at the table nearest the door and survey the handsome room. From that vantage point I can imagine it filled with students and teachers as they dig into fish and parsley-buttered potatoes or chicken and rice. I can see the chopped lettuce salad that one of Janet Hawksley's students said was like the earth because every piece seemed to be connected to every other making it difficult to spoon onto plates. I remember pea-sized portions and the cheerful buzz of voices and clink of flatware that provided the noon soundscape.

Now I shake my head and bring a different scene into my mind's eye. I'm still seated at the same corner table, but now it's 4:00 and the students have departed. The rest of the dining hall is clean and quiet, but the corner table is occupied by most of the staff, with chairs pulled up doubling the seating around the table. We have been lured from the papers that await correction and the lesson plans that require details by the plate in the center of the corner table, along with the coffee urn alongside. The plate might hold a pile of that day's dessert: Rice Krispy squares with fudge icing or brownies or chewy cookies. Sometimes, however, there would be a really special treat: the sort of cake or cookies that must have had a name back in Scotland or England. It would be rich with butter, and feature raspberry jam or marzipan, and we would polish it off with sips of coffee and surreptitiously lick our fingers when we were done. Each sweet offering seemed like a friendly message from Mrs. Leslie to us, though she had departed hours earlier.

I always thought the conversations that took place around that table were the true heart of Brookside. There were plenty of extraneous conversations, but we would shift and share successful strategies for puzzling students, discuss classroom remarks and what we could glean from them, describe upsetting incidents, and hear each other's opinions. From these discussions we would gain other perspectives and methods to enhance our own, and none of it would have happened without Flora Leslie's delectable treats!

Susan Rice

I always loved lunch with Mrs. Leslie and Mrs. Atfield during my 31 years at Brookside. I enjoyed the sound of the Lower School children playing outside the lunch windows, near the brook, during their afternoon recess (I always ate at the last lunch). I enjoyed the special lunches with singing and birthdays. I remember how special lunches were when we came back to school from outside physical education classes in the winter (snow sliders runs from the valley, Ram's Horn and the Brookside hill across the road).

Don Brown

The teachers and students always looked forward to the lunches at Brookside that were lovingly prepared by Flora Leslie. I loved to peek into the kitchen to have a cheery chat with Flora. Her smile and her very special Scottish way of speaking was very uplifting to me.

Gloria Lusk

While teaching Fourth Grade at Brookside, one of the events that I had to learn to accept was the appearance in class of Sebastian, the four and a half foot long bull snake, draped around the neck of one of my students. As I remember it, there were several students who coveted this privilege granted by Janet Hawksley. It was a real challenge for everyone, students and teacher, to concentrate on anything other than Sebastian's response to history and English which was merely serpentine indifference. But once upon a time, Sebastian took leave of his predictable environment and could not be found anywhere. For days there was no sign of him, and all were concerned and interested and fearful that he might have come to some harm. Eventually, however, he was found exactly where any smart snake would be — in Flora Leslie's flour drawer. The cool and cushioned bed must have been a pleasant change from being passed around from one neck to the other. Cookies, on the other hand, clearly had a new added spice.

Joan Page O'Hara

Flora Leslie's Beginnings At Brookside
In Her Own Words

I came from Scotland in 1930. I was in Scotland 22 years. I worked in a photographer's office. When I came over here you couldn't find work, it was depression years. I couldn't find work so I finally went to work for a family who were very interested in Cranbrook, the Wards. I came across them very suddenly.

On coming over here we had quite a terrible trip. It was very stormy, the month of December and none of us could go upstairs on the ship. So we stayed downstairs and talked to each other. I met this lady Mrs. Ward and I told her what I was trying to do when I came over here. Well she said if you don't find work, come and see me. And I couldn't find work and my uncle called her and I went out to Orchard Lake to see her.

Now they lived on Orchard Lake in a beautiful big, big old home. It was built by Mr. Henry Ward, Mr. Ward's grandfather. I lived there for one summer and I lived there one winter and then next summer they took me up to Hessel Michigan, and that was in 1931.

I always wanted to come to either Canada or the United states. And my mother said, "well you can try it for one year if you don't like it you can come home." I never went back.

I came to Cranbrook in 1932. I worked a year for Mrs. Ward and I came to Cranbrook. It was through Mrs. Ward that I came to Cranbrook. The depression came and people didn't have money and I worked for her, there were 7 of us who worked there. And she couldn't pay our salaries and she asked me if I would like to work in a girls' school.

I said yes, I would love to. So she sent a letter to Miss Adams, that was the headmistress then. And I started work at Kingswood. It was lovely. It was beautiful. Mr. Booth and Mr. Saarinen, they used to come every month and go through that whole place and anything they said that had to be added was added. Because by that time it was nearly all completed. And it was lovely because right across from our rooms was a nice field and a stream going through it. We used to go there and pick watercress. It was gorgeous we used to love to go at night when we were through working and pick watercress for the cook.

I was a dining room waitress. There were six people at each table and the waitress had two tables. And that was two tables she was responsible for. And it changed every two weeks, they changed us all over the place. At night there was a teacher at every table because in those days we only had 36 boarders.

We wore uniforms I hated those things. It was a gray uniform with a white collar, white apron and white cuffs. Mrs. Hyde was the dietician. And at the end of every two weeks we had to stand up in the kitchen and show our hands to be sure our nails were just right and everything. Can you imagine that today?

I went out at 7 in the morning. The girls came in at 8 we had to set up all the tables and have it all ready for them when they came in. So they came in at 8:00 AM and by 8:30 AM they were gone again. And we cleared the tables. There was a man in the kitchen who swept the floors, we only washed the tables and took everything off and then we set up again at 11:00 AM for a 1:00 PM lunch.

But we served orange juice every day at 10:00 AM in the terrace. If it was a nice sunny day we took it out in the sunshine and when it was dull we took it to the basement to the gym. We had lovely fresh orange juice all squeezed and poured into glasses and we carried the trays to where it was needed. My goodness today they would look at you and say where's the coca cola?! And you know we used to have fresh flowers at the beginning when I was there. Fresh flowers for the tables twice a week were delivered for that dining room.

I was at Kingswood two years. I was married while I lived at Kingswood. My husband worked at Kingswood. We were married in April 1934. My husbands name was George, I was Flora McFarland in Alexandria Scotland. After we were married we rented a little house in Birmingham. We were there three months when we came to Brookside. Now Jessie winters sent for us and asked us would we be interested. I wanted to see Brookside first. When I went down to see Brookside I didn't like it because it was old English, everything was dark. Kingswood was just so light and bright and lovely. We said we'd think about it. She said we had three months to think about I and she'd be in touch with us.

So one day my husband came and then he said, "you better get dressed Miss Winter wants to see us." So when we went back out to see Jessie about the job she had a little apartment all beautifully done up and I couldn't say no. And what really took me to Brookside was a Frigidaire. In those days people didn't have Frigidaires they had ice boxes. And when I went to the Brookside apartment here sat a brand new Frigidaire. I said we'll come. That's the truth. And it's still sitting in my garage, they gave it to me when I left the school.

When we first went there, there were only 50 children and three people did the work and at that time I did most of the cooking.

I do remember one famous resident, that was Charles Lindberg. I didn't meet him, I met his wife. She was a lovely lady and of course the children were just children you know, And they used to walk to school and she said it was the first time in their lives they were ever able to walk without people asking them who they were. But the children used to walk to school and Ann used to sometimes meet them, but she said it was the nicest time of her life living around Cranbrook.

Oh there's hundreds of stories, but I thought it was really funny the time when the bananas went a-missing. Well, I used to buy bananas from Mr. Wooding on Friday. And they'd have to stand out until Monday before they were ripe enough to use them. So, I had bought the bananas and I left them outside the store room so they would get ripe. The storeroom was cold and I put them outside. So Monday morning came and I noticed the bananas were missing. I went and told Jessie Winter, I said, "You know something's happened to the bananas, there's a lot of them missing and I don't have enough for this lunch."

She said, "We'll soon find out who did it, who do you think did it?" I said, "Well I think first graders, that's where they were down there by their door." So, she called all the boys in the first grade and asked them if they knew anything about the bananas. Yes they knew about the bananas. So at lunchtime she took them into the dining room and she lined them all up, all the boys. Now she said, "Each one of you tell the school why you took that banana, what was the story about the banana." Well one child would say he just took it because he wanted a banana. And it went right along the whole line until they came to the last one. And his father, his name was Hyde, his father was a business manager at Cranbrook. so he stepped up from the crowd and said, "Yes," he said, "yes I had a banana," and he said, "I'll tell you, they had no business there in the first place."

So Jesse didn't know what to say. I've seen her in a lot of little spots like that. And the same little boy gave her another hassle one day. And after she was through with him, she said, Flora we must never worry about this country when it's in the hands of boys like that.

But you know what he did, he was a slow eater. And everybody was gone and he was still eating. And Jesse was in the dining room eating her food. So she went over and said to him, "Why Andy, why are you so slow. Everybody's gone but you." He said, "I know." She said, "why is that?" He said, "Because I'm a slow eater." And she said, "Well I think you should just hurry up." And she said, "You know I don't think you're quite right, you're talking back to me." He said, "am I?" She said, "Yes." She said, "I thought you and I were very good friends, aren't we?" He said, "Yes, but friends talk that way to each other." And she didn't know what to say because she was getting deeper in and couldn't get out of it. So she finally said, "Well are we going to shake hands on this and be friends?" "No," he said, "I was sitting here eating my food, you're the one who started it."

Oh, he was something, he was only a young boy and she didn't what to say she was dumbfounded.

Mrs. Leslie's introduction was transcribed from an audio interview with Mrs. Flora Leslie by Mark Coir of the Cranbrook Archives on November 5, 1987. Interview courtesy of John Leslie and Mark Coir.

Harold Smart is not only known as Brookside's Art teacher for 42 years, but students will always remember Harold picking up a guitar after lunch and leading the lunchroom in song. Here are the lyrics of two of his most memorable numbers.

What Shall We Do With A Drunken Sailor

Note that "early" is often pronounced as "earl-eye."

Intro
What shall we do with a drunken sailor, (3×)
Early in the morning?
Chorus
Heave-ho and up she rises, (3×)
Early in the morning.
Verses
Put him in the longboat and make him bail 'er, (3×)
Early in the morning.
Put him in the bilge and make him drink it, (3x)
Early in the morning.
Pull out the plug and wet him all over, (3×)
Early in the morning.
Put him in the scuppers with a hosepipe on him, (3×)
Early in the morning.
Heave him by the leg in a running bowline, (3×)
Early in the morning.
Soak 'im in oil 'till he sprouts flippers, (3×)
Early in the morning.
Take him and shake him and try to wake him, (3×)
Early in the morning.
Tie him to the taffrail when she's yardarm under, (3×)
Early in the morning.
Keelhaul him, keelhaul him (3×)
Early in the morning.
Put him into bed with the captain's daughter,(*) (3×)
Early in the morning.
Make him shave with a rusty razor, (3×)
Early in the morning.
Put him in the back of the paddywagon, (3×)
Early in the morning.
Put him in his bunk with his pants on backwards, (3×)
Early in the morning.
Hang him from the yard-arm by his toe nails, (3x)
Early in the morning.
Send him down to Davy Jones locker, (3x)
Early in the morning.
Outro
That's what we'll do with a drunken sailor, (3×)
Early in the morning.

*The Captains Daughter was the other name for the cat o' nine-tails whip.

The Cat Came Back

Lyrics

Old Mister Johnson had troubles of his own
He had a yellow cat which wouldn't leave its home;
He tried and he tried to give the cat away,
He gave it to a man goin' far, far away.

Chorus

But the cat came back the very next day,
The cat came back, we thought he was a goner
But the cat came back; it just couldn't stay away.
Away, away, yea, yea, yea

Verses

The man around the corner swore he'd kill the cat on sight,
He loaded up his shotgun with nails and dynamite;
He waited and he waited for the cat to come around,
Ninety seven pieces of the man is all they found.

He gave it to a little boy with a dollar note,
Told him for to take it up the river in a boat;
They tied a rope around its neck, it must have weighed a pound
Now they drag the river for a little boy that's drowned.

He gave it to a man going up in a balloon,
He told him for to take it to the man in the moon;
The balloon came down about ninety miles away,
Where he is now, well I dare not say.

He gave it to a man going way out West,
Told him for to take it to the one he loved the best;
First the train hit the curve, then it jumped the rail,
Not a soul was left behind to tell the gruesome tale.

The cat it had some company one night out in the yard,
Someone threw a boot-jack, and they threw it mighty hard;
It caught the cat behind the ear, she thought it rather slight,
When along came a brick-bat and knocked the cat out of sight

Away across the ocean they did send the cat at last,
Vessel only out a day and making water fast;
People all began to pray, the boat began to toss,
A great big gust of wind came by and every soul was lost.

On a telegraph wire, sparrows sitting in a bunch,
The cat was feeling hungry, thought she'd like 'em for a lunch;
Climbing softly up the pole, and when she reached the top,
Put her foot upon the electric wire, which tied her in a knot.

The cat was a possessor of a family of its own,
With seven little kittens till there came a cyclone;
Blew the houses all apart and tossed the cat around,
The air was full of kittens, and not a one was ever found.

The atom bomb fell just the other day,
The H-Bomb fell in the very same way;
Russia went, England went, and then the U.S.A.
The human race was finished without a chance to pray.

But the cat came back the very next day,
The cat came back, we thought he was a goner
But the cat came back; it just couldn't stay away.
Away, away, yea, yea, yea

Favorite Recipes

From

Brookside School Cranbrook
REVISED EDITION

FAVORITE RECIPES

FROM

BROOKSIDE SCHOOL CRANBROOK

•

RECIPES
MRS. FLORA LESLIE, Dietitian
THE PARENTS AND TEACHERS

•

DRAWINGS
BY
THE CHILDREN OF
BROOKSIDE SCHOOL CRANBROOK
BLOOMFIELD HILLS, MICHIGAN

REVISED EDITION — SECOND PRINTING
APRIL, 1970
REVISED EDITION - THIRD PRINTING
APRIL, 2007

CO-CHAIRMEN

MRS. DAVID G. BOOTH   MRS. G. BRETNELL WILLIAMS

COMMITTEE

MRS. JAMES C. HOLMES   MRS. WILLIAM L. MITCHELL
MRS. ROBERT L MARTIN   MRS. RICHARD A. JONES
         MRS. ROBERT SCHOENFELD

PRINTED BY THE CRANBROOK PRESS
BLOOMFIELD HILLS, MICHIGAN

SINCE its inception less than two years ago, the Parents' Council has striven to bring Brookside and its philosophy of education closer to all the parents. With their assistance, the school has been able to function far more effectively.

Now, under the energetic guidance of Mrs. William L. Mitchell, the Parents' Council Chairman, and Mesdames David G. Booth and G. Bretnell Williams, the Council has assembled a collection of unusual and favorite recipes for a Brookside Cook Book. The proceeds from the sale of this book will support the activities of the Council in its increasingly important and active role in the life of our school.

I should like to dedicate this, their first enterprise, to the ladies, past, present, and future of the Parents' Council of Brookside School Cranbrook in appreciation of their untiring efforts on its behalf.

John P. Denio
Headmaster

April, 1964

FOREWORD

The Parents' Council is eternally grateful to Mrs. Flora Leslie for so generously sharing her special recipes. Some have been favorites of the Brookside children for many of the thirty years that she has been preparing the meals at our school. Other recipes are party delicacies that Mrs. Leslie has found most popular in our community. All are her own creations.

We sincerely thank her for sharing these culinary secrets with us. We bless her for her patience in reducing a recipe for two hundred people to a family-size casserole for eight!

Under the direction of Mr. Harold D. Smart, Jr., our art classes made a special project of creating the cover page and the dividers for each category. We are extremely proud of their work and thank them for their original contributions, and Mr. Smart for his skillful development of this project.

A word about the recipes contributed by the Brookside parents and teachers: every recipe has been tested by the donor and carefully checked by the cook book committee for ingredients, measurements and cooking time.

We hope you will enjoy these special recipes and repeat them often with pleasure.

Marian S. Mitchell
Parents' Council Chairman

CONTENTS

Page Number

Hors d'Oeuvres	1
Beverages	5
Soups and Sauces	7
Salads and Salad Dressings	11
Casseroles	19
Vegetables	31
Meats, Poultry and Fish	37
Sandwiches	45
Breads	47
Cookies	53
Desserts	61
Additional Recipes from Mrs. Flora Leslie	79
Index	83

Patty Daniels V

AVOCADO DIP

1 large or 2 small very ripe avocadoes, mashed
1 heaping teaspoon mayonnaise
2 teaspoons lemon juice or 1 teaspoon white vinegar
1 tablespoon finely chopped onion
1 drop Worchestershire sauce
Salt and pepper to taste

Mix above ingredients together. Serve with corn chips. Put in air tight container if made few hours ahead.

—Mrs. A. William Reynolds, II

CHEESE BISCUITS

2 cups flour
1/2 cup butter
1 teaspoon baking powder
1/4 teaspoon salt
1/2 cup grated sharp Cheddar cheese
1/3 cup and 1 tablespoon commercial sour cream
2 egg yolks
2 teaspoons water
Parmesan cheese
Paprika

Mix flour and butter with fingers until well blended and crumbly. Add baking powder, salt and cheese. Stir with fork until blended. Add sour cream gradually, stirring with fork. Knead lightly in bowl until dough clings and forms a ball. Pat a portion of dough to 1/2 inch thickness on a lightly floured board. Cut into 1 inch diameter rounds. Place on a cookie sheet. Brush tops with egg yolks beaten with water. Sprinkle with grated Parmesan cheese and a dash of paprika. Bake at 400° for approximately 12 minutes.
Serve biscuits warm as hors d'oeuvres. Makes about 40 bite size biscuits. May be frozen and rewarmed.

—Mrs. Louis A. Beer

CHEESE PASTRY WITH ANCHOVIES

Milk
1 cup flour
1/2 cup butter
1/4 teaspoon salt
1 cup grated American or Cheddar cheese
Anchovy fillets

Mix above ingredients together well, omitting the anchovies. Add enough milk to form a stiff dough. Roll thin. Cut into approximately 3 inch strips. Lay 1 anchovy fillet on each strip and fold pastry over to cover. Press sides together. Chill in refrigerator several hours. Just before serving bake in hot oven at 400° until brown.

—Mrs. Richard A. Jones

CLAM DIP
(Prepare two days in advance)

2 10-ounce cans well drained, minced clams (reserve juice)
12 ounces cream cheese, softened
1 large clove garlic, minced as finely as possible
2 heaping tablespoons grated onion
2 teaspoons lemon juice
3 ounces sour cream
2 teaspoons Worcestershire sauce
1 teaspoon Tabasco sauce
1 teaspoon salt
Large dash of black pepper

Put all contents in mixing bowl and mince with heavy fork. From time to time add enough clam juice to bring to proper dip consistency. Decorate with paprika. Cover and refrigerate (not freeze) for at least 2 days. If too stiff to dip when serving, thin carefully with more clam juice. My special formula. Serves 40.

—Dr. Lynn N. Hershey

LIVER SPREAD

1 8-ounce package cream cheese
1 8-ounce liver sausage roll
1 teaspoon onion, finely grated
Few dashes Tabasco sauce
Few dashes Worcestershire sauce
Few dashes salt

Soften sausage and cream cheese; blend together well. Add onion, Tabasco sauce, Worcestershire sauce and salt. Mold into a long roll, wrap in plastic wrap and harden in refrigerator. Frost with cream cheese mixture.

Frosting

1 3-ounce package cream cheese
Cream
Parsley, chopped
Paprika

Soften cream cheese; add a little cream so that it will spread. Then frost the hardened roll. Sprinkle the top with parsley and paprika. Serve after roll has been at room temperature for about $1/2$ hour. Surround the roll with fancy cocktail crackers.

—Mrs. William L. Mitchell

WASHINGTON, D.C. DIP

1 jar red caviar
1 one pound carton Spring cottage cheese (herbs have been added)

Mix and serve with crackers of your choice. Delectable and easy.

—Mrs. Robert V. Hackett

SHRIMP SPREAD

1½ envelopes unflavored gelatin
½ cup cold water
1 can tomato soup, hot
1 large or 2 small packages cream cheese
1 cup salad dressing
2 5-ounce cans shrimp, cut very fine, crosswise
Salt
Pepper
¾ cup finely chopped onion
¾ cup finely chopped celery
Stuffed green olives, chopped fine

Dissolve gelatin in cold water. Add hot soup and stir until dissolved. While still warm add cream cheese, salad dressing, shrimp, salt and pepper to taste. When cool but not set add onion, celery and olives. If used as cocktail spread take from refrigerator one hour before serving. If used as a salad dressing on wedge of lettuce serve at once. Makes 2 bread pan size molds. Very, very good. Try at next party.

—Dr. Lynn N. Hershey

MUSHROOM ROLLS FOR COCKTAIL PARTIES

1 pound mushrooms, fresh only (stems too)
3 tablespoons butter
2 tablespoons flour
¼ cup cream
½ teaspoon onion juice
Dash of nutmeg
Loaf of unsliced white bread

Wipe mushrooms and put through meat grinder and sauté in butter. Cook altogether until thick enough to spread. Spread on thin sliced bread and roll. Spread outside of roll with butter and toast under broiler until nice and brown. Serves 8 to 10. We do not use these at school. I thought some of the parents would like to have this recipe.

—**Mrs. Flora Leslie**

MINIATURE MOCK PIZZAS

English muffins
Butter
Catsup
Lebanon bologna
Olives
Mushrooms, sliced canned
Cheese

Split English muffins, butter and spread with catsup. Put slice of bologna on each half, decorate with small olive halves, mushrooms and strips of cheese. You may do this ahead of time and put in refrigerator. Just before serving put pizzas under the broiler for a few minutes. Cut in four wedges.

—Mrs. Ben M. Snyder

SWEET-SOUR SPARE-RIB BITES

3 pounds small lean spare-ribs. Have butcher cut the ribs crosswise so each piece is about two inches long.
½ lemon
½ cup finely chopped onion, medium
Salt
Pepper

Heat oven to 450°. Separate ribs by cutting between each rib with kitchen shears. Place pieces of rib in shallow baking pan. Sprinkle lightly with salt and pepper, but do not cover or add water. Cut lemon into very thin slices; then into quarters. Sprinkle lemon and onion over meat. Roast for 45 minutes. Pour sweet-sour sauce over ribs and reduce heat to 350°. Continue baking for one hour. Baste with sauce about every 15 minutes. If sauce gets too thick, add a little hot water. Serves 12 to 16.

Sweet-Sour Sauce

½ teaspoon chili powder
½ teaspoon salt
Dash pepper
1½ teaspoons celery seeds
2 tablespoons brown sugar
Few drops Tabasco sauce if desired
2 tablespoons vinegar
2 tablespoons Worcestershire sauce
½ cup catsup
½ cup water

Mix all ingredients and bring to a boil. This is very good and can be made in advance and frozen.

—Dr. Leonard Latos

PINK ZIP

¾ cup mayonnaise
¼ cup milk
¼ teaspoon salt
Dash cayenne pepper
2 tablespoons catsup
½ teaspoon grated lemon rind
1 tablespoon lemon juice
½ cup sour cream

Combine mayonnaise, milk, salt and cayenne in small pan. Heat slowly, stirring constantly, just until hot. Remove from heat. Stir in catsup, lemon rind and juice. Fold in cream. Heat until warm. Serve over vegetables.

—Mrs. James C. Holmes

Beverages

IRISH COFFEE
...in five easy steps

1. Fill a pre-heated glass to within one-half inch of the brim with hot black coffee.
2. Drop one or more cocktail cubes of sugar into coffee (according to taste).
3. Stir until completely dissolved.
4. Add one jigger of Irish whiskey.
5. Spread lightly whipped cream over a spoon, so that THE CREAM FLOATS on the top. Don't stir. Drink through the cream. Indescribably luscious!

—Miss Martha E. Ratliff

PUNCH

6 large (14 ounce) cans of grapefruit-pineapple juice
1 6-ounce can of frozen lime juice (3 cans of water)
1 6-ounce can of frozen lemonade (3 cans of water)
1 8-ounce cup fruit punch base
1 quart of water
1 large bottle of port wine
2-3 cups gin

Pour punch over heart-shaped mold of ice with thin slices of fresh lime, maraschino cherries (green and red), and green grapes in season.

—Mrs. G. Bretnell Williams

ORANGE SHERBET PUNCH

2 large cans pineapple juice
2 large cans apricot juice
2 large cans tangerine juice
  (MOST IMPORTANT)
3 quarts gingerale or more
½ gallon orange sherbet
Floating frozen strawberries

Have everything chilled first. Mix ingredients in large punch bowl and serve. Will serve between 15 and 20. If using ice cubes make stronger. Wonderful with champagne, too.

—Mrs. Roy A. Fruehauf

ST. DUNSTAN'S CHRISTMAS PUNCH

3 quarts sparkling water
3 fifths extra-dry champagne
3 fifths sparkling red burgundy
1 fifth brandy

Pour the above over a cake of ice in a large punch bowl. Serve when thoroughly chilled. Makes 70 punch cup size servings. This sparkling red punch is served at the annual Christmas Party to the members of St. Dunstan's Guild of Cranbrook.

—Mr. Stephen F. Booth

EGG NOG GENTRY

8 eggs
1 cup confectioners sugar
1 pint milk
1 quart vanilla ice cream
¾ bottle Grand Marnier
¾ bottle Jamaica rum
½ bottle brandy
4 ponies crème de cacao

Separate yolks from whites. Beat yolks with sugar until light and frothy. Slowly stir in remainder of ingredients, then fold in stiffly beaten egg whites. Stir well. Serve in punch bowl. Top with nutmeg when serving. Yield: 1 gallon.

—Mrs. Robert G. Wild

SASSAFRAS TEA

Bring 3 quarts of water to a boil. Add a piece of sassafras root four inches long and an inch thick. Add sugar to taste. Allow to steep about five minutes and you will have a drink resembling hot root beer.

—Mrs. Janet M. Hawksley

APPLE-ONION SOUP

2 onions
2 apples
2 cans consommé, undiluted
½ pint light cream
Dash of curry
Dash sour cream

Peel and cut up onions and apples. Boil in consommé until soft enough to push through sieve. Add cream to apple-onion-consommé mixture and a dash of curry to taste. May be served hot or cold. If serving cold add a dash of sour cream just before serving. Simple and delicious. Serves 8.

—Mrs. Robert W. Chambers

BEAN SOUP

¼ pound butter
3 tablespoons flour (generous)
1 clove garlic, chopped fine
1 teaspoon tomato paste
1 quart cold stock or consommé and water
1-2 cans cooked dry butter or lima beans or
1 pound of dried beans soaked in water overnight
Salt
Pepper
Paprika

Make choux: (Melt butter. Put in flour and cook until it turns golden brown.) Remove from fire. Add garlic and tomato paste. Stir in cold stock and cook for a while; then add beans. Salt and pepper to taste. Add paprika. May be topped before serving with fried chopped onions, fresh chopped chives or chopped bacon.

—Mrs. Clifford B. West

CORN CHOWDER

5 slices bacon
1 1-pound can whole kernel corn
1 medium onion, thinly sliced
1 cup diced raw pared potatoes
½ teaspoon salt
1 can condensed cream of celery soup
1½ cups milk
Pepper

In large saucepan cook bacon until crisp. Remove bacon and reserve drippings. Drain corn reserving liquid. To bacon drippings in saucepan add reserved liquid, onions, potatoes and salt. Cover and simmer for 15 minutes or until tender. Add soup, milk and corn, heat through. Season to taste with salt and pepper. Crumble bacon over chowder. If desired drop in a pat of butter.

—Mrs. Stephen F. Booth

OXTAIL SOUP

1 oxtail
2 onions
1/4-1/2 cup red wine

Brown onions in small amount of bacon fat. Remove from pan. Salt oxtail, brush with flour and brown on all sides in same pan. Return onions to pan and add enough water to completely cover meat. Simmer in covered pan for 3 1/2 hours. (In pressure cooker time is 2 hours at 10 pounds pressure).
After cooking, separate meat from bone. Put soup broth through sieve to remove onions. Bring broth to boil, thicken with flour and water paste. Add meat pieces.
Add 1/4 - 1/2 cup wine depending on taste. Serves 4.
This soup is thick, full of flavor and when served with rolls, is a meal in itself.

—Mrs. Robert J. Schoenfeld

GREEN PEA SOUP

2 cups chicken broth
2 packages frozen peas
1 sliced onion
1 sliced carrot
2 lettuce leaves
3 tablespoons butter
1 cup cream
Salt and pepper
Pinch of ginger
Croutons, fried in butter

Cook peas, onion, carrot and lettuce leaves in broth until tender. Put in blender and blend well. Pour into top of double boiler and heat. Add remaining ingredients. Serve topped with fried croutons.

—Mrs. Richard A. Jones

TOMATO WIENER SOUP
A La Fritz Hershey and Several Brookside Classmates

2 cans condensed tomato soup, diluted with two cans milk
1 commercial package of your favorite wieners (skinless preferable) sliced into thin Flying Saucers

Heat over slow heat to prevent curdling. Do not reach boiling point. Complete meal when served with rolls. Under pressure from Brookside students you may have to offer popsicle or equivalent.

—Mrs. Spencer R. Hershey

U.S. SENATE SOUP

1 pound Navy beans, soaked overnight
2 quarts cold water
Ham bone
1 clove garlic, crushed
1 stalk celery
1 large carrot
1 - 2 bay leaves
1 shredded onion
1 stale heel of rye bread
1 chopped onion
Salt and pepper
1 cup mashed potatoes
3/4 cup finely chopped parsley
Half a garlic smoked bologna ring, cut into thumb nail size pieces

Cook first nine items on low heat for about 3 hours. Add chopped onion after browning in butter; also salt and pepper. In last hour of cooking remove carrot, celery and bay leaves. Cut meat off bone. Add enough water to make soup, not stew. Add potatoes, parsley and bologna. Stir well and continue cooking over low heat. Stir often.

—Dr. Lynn N. Hershey

TOMATO BOUILLON

1 can tomato soup
1 can beef bouillon
1 can water
1/4 cup dry sherry
1/4 teaspoon dried basil or parsley

Combine ingredients. Heat and serve with a slice of lemon in each cup. —Mrs. Charles F. Delbridge, Jr.

CHOCOLATE SAUCE

3/4 pound butter
6 cups confectioners sugar
2 cups evaporated milk
1 8-ounce package chocolate squares, grated
2 tablespoons vanilla

Melt butter and chocolate. Add remaining ingredients and cook for 30 minutes. —**Mrs. Flora Leslie**

MINT SAUCE

1/2 cup vinegar
1 cup sugar
1/2 cup finely chopped mint leaves

Bring vinegar and sugar to boil. Remove from heat. Add mint. Cover pan and let stand for one hour. Serve hot or cold.

—Mrs. James C. Holmes

MEAT SAUCE
(For Beef or Venison)

Mix together in top of double boiler equal amounts of:
- Red currant jelly
- Chili sauce or cocktail sauce
- Red cooking wine

Heat until blended and serve on hot or cold meat. Some people add butter, but that is fattening.

—Mrs. Francis C. McMath

MEAT SPAGHETTI SAUCE

1/4 cup olive oil	1 tablespoon sugar
2 tablespoons butter	2 bay leaves
2 large onions, chopped	Salt
2 cloves garlic, chopped	Peppercorns
1 pound ground stew beef	Oregano
1 6-ounce can tomato paste	Worcestershire sauce
1 No. 2 can tomatoes	(or your own condiments to suit
1/4 cup dry red wine	taste)

Sauté onion and garlic in oil and butter. When yellow add beef and cook until brown. Mix in order tomato paste, tomatoes, wine, sugar, salt, peppercorns, oregano, bay leaves and Worcestershire sauce. Bake in earthenware casserole for three hours covered tightly at 250°. Add additional tomato juice if needed. Serve over thin spaghetti with hand grated Romano cheese.

—Mrs. Henry L. Newnan, Jr.

MUSTARD SAUCE

1/2 cup sugar	1/2 cup vinegar
1 tablespoon flour	1 cup undiluted evaporated milk
2 tablespoons dry mustard	

Mix the sugar, flour and mustard thoroughly in top of double boiler. Stir in vinegar, then stir in the milk over heat. Cook until thickened stirring occasionally.

Serve hot or cold with meat or fish. Also good cold on sandwiches. Will keep indefinitely if placed in a tightly covered jar in the refrigerator.

—Mrs. Richard F. Jones

BEAN SALAD

1 can slender green beans
1 can yellow wax beans
1 can small green lima beans
1 can garbanzo beans
1 cup diced celery
Onion rings to taste
½ cup chopped green pepper
2 cups cauliflower flowerets
2 cups cider vinegar
½ cup water
1¾ cups sugar
1 tablespoon salt
½ clove garlic (may be left in over night only)

Drain liquids from beans and place in large bowl. Add celery, onions, green pepper, cauliflower and toss.
Combine vinegar, sugar, water and salt. Bring to a boil. Cool and pour over vegetables. Refrigerate at least 24 hours.
—Mrs. David P. Williams

JELLIED CARROT AND PINEAPPLE SALAD

2 packages lime flavored gelatin
2 cups hot water (dissolve)
2 cups pineapple juice
1 No. 2 can crushed pineapple
1 cup finely shredded carrots

Makes 1 large molded salad or 12 individual salads.
—Mrs. Flora Leslie

COLE SLAW

1 large new cabbage, shredded fine
¼ cup sugar
1 teaspoon salt
¼ cup grated onion
2 tablespoons vinegar

Mix well and add 1 cup prepared salad dressing. Choose a nice green cabbage for this slaw. Serves 8 to 10.
—Mrs. Flora Leslie

BLACK CHERRY SALAD
(Special for parents)

1 large can pitted black cherries (put a pecan in each cherry)
2 packages lemon flavored gelatin
1 cup cherry juice
2 cups port wine
1 cup boiling water

Makes 1 large molded or 12 individual salads. Serve on bib lettuce leaf with celery seed dressing.
—Mrs. Flora Leslie

CHERRY CREAM RING

1 package lime flavored gelatin	1 3-ounce package cream cheese
1 package lemon flavored gelatin	2 tablespoons mayonnaise
1 can Queen Anne cherries or white cherries	1 small can crushed pineapple, drained

Drain and pit cherries and arrange in four cup ring mold. Prepare lime gelatin as directed on package and pour over cherries. Chill until set. Blend softened cream cheese and mayonnaise until smooth. Prepare lemon gelatin as directed on package and combine with pineapple, cream cheese and mayonnaise. Cool slightly and pour over first layer. There is almost a cup of mixture left over for an additional small mold. Chill at least three hours. Serves 8 to 10.

—Mrs. Harold D. Smart, Jr.

CHICKEN PERFECTION ASPIC

1 envelope unflavored gelatin	1/2 cup finely shredded cabbage
1 cup cold water	1/4 cup chopped celery
1 can condensed consommé	1/4 cup chopped green pepper
1/4 teaspoon salt	1/4 cup chopped pimento
5 ounce can boned chicken or turkey	2 tablespoons lemon juice

Sprinkle gelatin on one half cup cold water to soften, place over boiling water and stir until dissolved. Add remaining water, consommé, salt and lemon juice. Chill until mixture is consistency of unbeaten egg white. Fold in chicken, cabbage, pepper and pimento. Turn into 4 cup mold and chill until firm.

—Dr. Lynn N. Hershey

HOT CHICKEN SALAD

1 cup mayonnaise	1/2 cup chopped salted almonds
2 tablespoons lemon juice	1 red pimento, cut into strips
1 teaspoon scraped onion	2/3 cup crushed potato chips
2 cups diced cooked chicken	1/2 cup grated cheese
2 cups diced celery	

Combine mayonnaise, lemon juice and onion. Add chicken, celery, almonds and pimento and stir lightly. Turn into casserole and sprinkle top with potato chips and cheese. Bake at 350° for 1/2 hour or until brown. Serves 6.

—Mrs. David G. Booth

MARTHA'S SALAD

1 envelope unflavored gelatin	Juice of 1 lemon
1 package lemon flavored gelatin	4 slices pineapple, diced
1/2 cup cold water	1 small can pimento, cut up
2 cups boiling water	1/2 bottle tiny pearl onions
1/2 cup pineapple juice	2 tablespoons capers
1/2 cup sugar	

Dissolve unflavored gelatin in cold water. Dissolve lemon flavored gelatin in boiling water. Mix together and add pineapple juice and sugar. Pour into 1 quart salad mold and let thicken a little.

Add the pineapple, pimento, onions and capers. Stir lightly to mix the pieces. Serves 8.

—Miss Martha E. Ratliff

MOLDED CINNAMON SALAD

2 packages black cherry flavored gelatin	1/2 cup red cinnamon candies
2 1/2 cups boiling water	2 cups apple sauce

Dissolve gelatin in boiling water. Add candies immediately, stir and crush until completely dissolved. Allow gelatin to cool. Add applesauce and pour into mold. Serves 8 to 10.

—Mrs. Harold D. Smart, Jr.

MOLDED CRAB MEAT SALAD

1 can tomato soup plus 2 tablespoons water	3 tablespoons celery, chopped fine
1 large package cream cheese	2 tablespoons onion, chopped fine
2 envelopes unflavored gelatin	3 tablespoons green olives or green pepper, chopped fine
1/2 cup cold water	2 cups crab meat or lobster
1 cup mayonnaise	

Heat to a rolling boil tomato soup mixed with water. Remove from heat and add cream cheese. Beat until smooth with electric beater. Add gelatin which has been softened with cold water. Beat in mayonnaise. Add celery, onion and olives or green pepper. Then add crab meat or lobster. Place in a ring mold or individual molds. Chill. Serve on lettuce. Garnish with cucumber, tomato and ripe olives. May be made the day before. This served with hot buttered rolls is my specialty for luncheon.

—Mrs. John J. Marra

FROZEN CRANBERRY SALAD

1 can whole cranberries
1 can crushed pineapple (drained)
½ pint sour cream
½ cup chopped nuts

Mix ingredients and put in refrigerator tray in freezer.
—Mrs. Philip E. Lachman

JELLIED CUCUMBER SALAD

4 packages lime flavored gelatin
1 teaspoon salt
⅓ cup sugar
4 cups hot water
2 cups pineapple juice
½ cup lime juice
¼ cup vinegar
4½ cups grated cucumber (4 medium)
2 cups finely diced cucumber (2 medium)

Dissolve gelatin, salt and sugar in hot water. Add pineapple juice, lime juice, vinegar and grated cucumber and chill until slightly thickened. Sprinkle diced cucumber with a little salt and fold into slightly thickened gelatin. Pour into three quart ring mold and chill until firm.

Center may be filled with seafood. Serve with mayonnaise dressing flavored to taste, with mustard or mustard powder, salt and pepper. —Mrs. G. Bretnell Williams

FAUCON SALAD

Crisp salad greens
Sliced hard boiled eggs
Crumbled crisp bacon
Creamy Roquefort Dressing

Place a substantial bed of greens in individual bowls and then a layer of eggs. Top with dressing and sprinkle liberally with bacon.

Creamy Roquefort Dressing

6 ounces Roquefort cheese
1 cup mayonnaise
1 cup cream
Juice of one medium lemon

Mash cheese and stir in remaining ingredients.
—Mrs. Charles F. Delbridge, Jr.

RUBY SALAD

2 packages of strawberry flavored gelatin
Sections of 6 grapefruit
½ pound green seedless grapes
3 cups water

Makes 1 large mold. Serve on bib lettuce or watercress. The children like this salad. Serves 8 to 10. —Mrs. Flora Leslie

GELATIN SALAD

1 package lemon flavored gelatin
1 cup hot water
1 can stewed tomatoes (No. 303)
Chopped onion to taste
2 tablespoons wine vinegar
1 teaspoon Worcestershire sauce
2 drops Tabasco sauce
Salt and pepper

Dissolve gelatin in hot water. Add remaining ingredients. Pour into mold and chill. You may add avocado.

—Mrs. James C. Holmes

GREEN GRAPE SALAD

1 tablespoon unflavored gelatin soaked in
1/2 cup cold water
1 cup boiling water
1/2 cup sugar
Few grains salt
1/2 cup lime juice
1 bunch grapes (remove seeds)

Dissolve gelatin in boiling water. Add sugar, salt, and lime juice. Chill until it begins to set and stir in grapes. Chill until set. Serves 5 to 6.

—Mrs. G. Bretnell Williams

TOSSED GREEN SALAD

1 head lettuce torn into small pieces
8 radishes, sliced
4 green onions, cut in strips
1 cucumber, sliced
Celery strips (1 bunch hearts)
2 carrots, cut in strips

We leave all the vegetables in groups on platter, dressing in the center. Small children like it better that way. From the Third Grade on we chop vegetables and mix with Italian dressing. Serves 8 to 10.

—Mrs. Flora Leslie

SAUERKRAUT MOLD

1 3-ounce package lemon flavored gelatin
1/2 cup boiling water
1 cup cold water
1/4 cup sour cream
1/2 cup sauerkraut, drained and chopped
1/3 cup raw apples, chopped
2 tablespoons onion, chopped fine
1/2 cup cucumber, coarsely grated

Mix first four ingredients and refrigerate until consistency of unbeaten egg whites. Add sauerkraut, apples, onion and cucumber. Refrigerate until firm. Garnish with cucumber slices and raw apples. Serve with a sour cream dressing.

—Mrs. William F. Thomas

ROMANO SALAD

Head of romaine
1 red onion, sliced
1/4 teaspoon summer savory
White vinegar
Vegetable oil
Onion salt
Coarse black pepper
Dash Worcestershire sauce
Romano cheese
Sliced tomato
Sliced avocado

Wash romaine. Shake out excess water, wrap in towel and place in refrigerator along with red onion and summer savory. Chill for at least 1 hour (or 15 minutes in freezer). Just before serving add tomato and avocado slices. Sprinkle, in order, with oil, onion salt, pepper, Worcestershire sauce, vinegar and hand grated Romano cheese. Toss lightly and serve.

—Mrs Henry L. Newnan, Jr.

STRAWBERRY SALAD

2 small packages strawberry flavored gelatin
2 small packages lemon flavored gelatin
4 small boxes frozen strawberries
1 small can crushed pineapple
2 cups boiling water

Add gelatin to boiling water; stir until thoroughly dissolved. Add frozen strawberries (do not thaw) and pineapple. Mix well and pour into 2 quart mold. Chill. Serve on bibb lettuce with sour cream dressing.

Sour Cream Dressing

1 pint commercial sour cream
30 miniature marshmallows

Fold marshmallows into sour cream. Put dressing in small dish in middle of strawberry salad mold. Serves 8 to 10.

—**Mrs. Flora Leslie**

ITALIAN SHRIMP SALAD

Bibb or butter lettuce
3 medium boiled potatoes, sliced
18 cooked shrimp, sliced in half
1 1/2 tablespoons capers
3 anchovy fillets, chopped
1 tablespoon lemon juice
3 tablespoons olive oil
1/4 cup mayonnaise
Salt and pepper to taste

Line a salad bowl with lettuce leaves. Add a layer of potatoes; then capers, anchovies and shrimp. Mix remaining ingredients and pour over top.

—Mrs. Charles F. Delbridge, Jr.

BUTTERMILK SALAD DRESSING

1 cup buttermilk
1 heaping teaspoon prepared mustard
5 heaping tablespoons salad dressing (similar to mayonnaise)
1 teaspoon salt
5 tablespoons cider vinegar
½ cup sugar

Mix all ingredients. Serve on greens or fruits.

—Mrs. A. William Reynolds, II

SPARKLING BURGUNDY SALAD DRESSING

Combine in large mixing bowl:

½ teaspoon salt
¼ teaspoon pepper
½ teaspoon mixed pickling spice (reduce to powder)
¼ teaspoon oregano
⅛ teaspoon garlic powder
¼ teaspoon sage
⅛ teaspoon curry powder

Add:

1 teaspoon Worcestershire sauce
½ teaspoon soy sauce
Few drops Tabasco sauce

Mix thoroughly using wire whip or beater.

Add:

2 ounces cream sherry
1 quart mayonnaise

Mix thoroughly and add:

2 ounces coffee cream
1 cup sparkling burgundy

Mix thoroughly. Allow to stand at room temperature for 30 minutes. Then refrigerate until ready to use.

—Mrs. Robert L. Martin

CELERY SEED SALAD DRESSING

½ cup sugar
1 teaspoon dry mustard
1 teaspoon salt
¼ cup grated onion
⅓ cup vinegar
1 cup salad oil
1 tablespoon celery seed

Mix the sugar, mustard, salt and grated onion. Add a bit of the vinegar to this dry mixture and blend thoroughly. Then add vinegar and oil alternately and beat well. Add the celery seed and mix again.

Store in refrigerator in a glass jar. Excellent on fruit salad.

—Miss Martha E. Ratliff

GREEN GODDESS DRESSING

Garlic	Tarragon leaves, chopped fine
8 - 10 fillets of anchovies	3 cups mayonnaise
1 piece of young onion	Tarragon vinegar
Parsley leaves, chopped fine	Chives, chopped fine

Rub bowl with garlic, or use a little garlic flavored oil. Mix anchovies, onion, parsley and tarragon leaves with mayonnaise; add a little vinegar and chives. Serve dressing mixed with the following cut greens, romaine, escarole and chicory.

—Mrs. Richard K. Scales

BEEF CASSEROLE

1 pound hamburger	1 teaspoon salt
2 tablespoons butter	1 teaspoon pepper
Garlic salt	1 tablespoon sugar

Sauté the above ingredients until the meat is brown.

Mix together:

2 8-ounce cans tomato sauce	1/2 package medium noodles, cooked and drained

Mix together:

3 or 4 green onions, chopped fine	3 ounce package cream cheese
	1 cup sour cream

Place the three mixtures in layers in a greased casserole, beginning with the noodles, then the sour cream mixture, lastly the meat. Use a shallow casserole. Sprinkle the top layer with Parmesan cheese. Heat thoroughly until bubbly. This dish is better when made the day before. Serves 6.

—Mrs. Calvert Thomas

CRAB MEAT CASSEROLE

7 ounces crab meat (frozen crab)	1 onion, grated
7 ounces shrimp	1 green pepper, cut up
1 cup mayonnaise	1 teaspoon Tabasco sauce
1 cup celery	

Mix all ingredients and bake in a shallow dish for 30 minutes at 300°. Serves about 4.

—Mrs. Ralph L. Polk, Jr.

HAMBURGER CASSEROLE

1 1/2 pounds hamburger	Pepper
2 onions	2 tablespoons soy sauce
1 1/4 cups diced celery	1 can cream of mushroom soup
1/2 cup uncooked rice	1 can cream of chicken soup
Salt	1 or 2 cans water

Brown hamburger with onions. Turn into casserole. Add remaining ingredients and bake at 350° about 1 1/2 hours until rice is entirely cooked. Serves 5 to 7.

This is particularly good and easy when you have an unexpected crowd and everything can be doubled for larger quantities.

—Mrs. Donald S. Mann

BEEF PROVENCAL

2 cloves of garlic
1½ pounds beef, cut in small pieces
½ cup flour, seasoned with:
2 teaspoons salt
½ teaspoon pepper and
¼ teaspoon thyme
2 tablespoons olive oil
2 cups dry white wine
1 bay leaf
1 stalk celery
8 ounce jar of pitted green olives

Cut garlic in small pieces. With skewer, punch a hole in each piece of meat, and insert a piece of garlic. Dredge the beef with seasoned flour. Brown meat in olive oil in a heavy pan. When pieces are brown on all sides, reduce heat and add wine, bay leaf and celery stalk. Simmer slowly for 2 hours, adding water, if necessary. Drain olives and cook in boiling water for 5 minutes to remove salt. Add olives to stew and simmer ½ hour more. Remove bay leaf and celery before serving.

Serve with buttered casserole of rice and grated Gruyère cheese in alternating layers. Serves 4 to 6.

—Mrs. Harold G. Schneider

BUFFET CASSEROLE

½ pound noodles
1 tablespoon butter
1 pound ground chuck beef
2 8-ounce cans tomato sauce
1 cup cottage cheese
1 8-ounce package cream cheese
¼ cup sour cream
⅓ cup minced scallions
1 tablespoon minced green pepper
2 tablespoons melted butter or margarine

Cook noodles as directed and drain. In a skillet melt butter and sauté ground chuck beef until browned. Stir in tomato sauce. Remove from heat. Combine cottage cheese, cream cheese, sour cream, scallions and green pepper. Spread half of the noodles in a two quart casserole. Cover with cheese mixture, then cover with the rest of the noodles. Pour butter over noodles. Then pour over the tomato meat sauce. Bake for 45 minutes at 375°.

—Mrs. Robert P. Patterson

CHICKEN CRAB CASSEROLE

3 cups cooked chicken, diced
2 7½-ounce cans crab meat
8 slices bacon
2 10-ounce packages frozen peas
6 tablespoons butter
6 tablespoons flour
1½ cups chicken broth
1½ teaspoons salt
¾ teaspoon paprika
1 small clove garlic, peeled, crushed
⅛ teaspoon nutmeg
5-6 drops liquid pepper seasoning
2¼ cups sour cream

Melt butter in double boiler. Stir in flour and add chicken broth gradually. Cook and stir until smooth and thickened. Add salt, paprika, garlic, nutmeg and liquid pepper. Cover and cook for 10-15 minutes, stirring occasionally. Add sour cream, mix well and continue heating over just simmering water. Add chicken and crab meat. Mix lightly. Heat for 10-15 minutes. Fry bacon crisp, drain on paper and crumble. Add to chicken and crab meat mixture. Put in serving dish, surround with peas. Serves 8.

—Mrs. G. Bretnell Williams

FABULOUS MERGER OF FLAVORS CASSEROLE

6 or 8 large, perfect slices of chicken or turkey breast (a few broad slivers permitted)
6 slices of boiled or baked ham ¼ inch thick (a few extra slivers permitted)
2 cans condensed cream of mushroom soup
6 to 10 beautiful, fresh mushroom caps sautéed in a little butter; set aside

Spread bottom of medium size casserole dish (without a cover) with a layer of undiluted mushroom soup. Over this lay a couple slices of ham, then slices of chicken or turkey. Cover with layer of mushroom soup. Continue until there are 2 or 3 layers total, topped with the remainder of mushroom soup. Top with sautéed mushroom caps along with butter and juice in sauté pan. Bake at 350° until heated through and the flavors of chicken or turkey, ham and mushrooms have blended. Will hold one hour or more, if the temperature is reduced to warm and the top is then protected against drying.

—Mrs. Spencer R. Hershey

FRANKFURTER CASSEROLE

1 pound frankfurters	Few parsley sprigs, chopped
2 tablespoons butter	2 cans (one pound size) red kidney beans
2 medium sized onions, sliced thinly	1/4 teaspoon salt
4 stalks celery, chopped coarsely	1-1 1/2 teaspoons curry powder

Cut frankfurters into quarters. Melt butter in skillet. Brown frankfurters and onion slices. Add celery and parsley along with undrained kidney beans, salt and curry powder. Stir well. Transfer to 1 1/2 quart casserole, cover and bake at 400°, for 1 hour.

Keeps well if dinner is delayed, and is a children's favorite with hot cornbread on the side. Serves 4.

—Mrs. Robert V. Hackett

LEFT-OVER DELIGHT WITH STUFFING

Stew base	Onions
Celery	Peas
Green pepper	Left-over meat
Fresh tomatoes	

Make a stew base using olive oil, flour and water or left-over gravy. Add vegetables such as celery, green pepper, fresh tomatoes, onions, peas, etc. Let the base simmer on stove for 3 or 4 hours. Just before serving add left-over meat such as chicken or roasts and heat thoroughly. Serve over stuffing. Serves 4 to 5.

STUFFING—Make one hour before serving

8 or 9 slices white bread, diced	1 stick of butter, melted
1 large onion, diced	2 eggs

Put bread into a large mixing bowl, adding the onions and toss together. Add eggs and butter and mix well. Keep adding hot water to this mixture until extremely moist. Wrap in foil and place in 350° oven for one hour. Serve stuffing as a base, with left-over stew on top. Tossed green salad on side helps make the dinner complete.

—Mrs. Charles S. Himelhoch

HAM, CHICKEN, BROCCOLI MORNAY

½ ham
1 capon
4 boxes frozen broccoli
Mornay sauce
Pimento slivers

Cook ham and chicken and slice very thinly. For individual servings, place several (2 or 3) slices ham, then 2 or 3 slices chicken, then crossed stalks broccoli in large flat baking dish or roaster insert. Cover with double recipe standard Mornay sauce. Heat before serving and garnish with crossed pimento slivers. Serves 8 amply.

Ham, chicken and sauce may all be cooked day before.

Mornay Sauce

Standard white sauce, plus 2 tablespoons butter and 2 tablespoons each of Parmesan and Swiss or other grated cheese per cup of sauce.

—Mrs. G. Bretnell Williams

MACARONI CASSEROLE

2 cups cooked macaroni
1 cup sharp cheese, cubed
½ cup diced onion
½ cup green pepper
1½ cups cubed boiled ham
2 cloves minced garlic (not salt)
1 can drained tomatoes

Mix all ingredients together. Place in greased casserole dish. Sprinkle generously with Parmesan cheese and paprika. Bake at 325° for 45 - 75 minutes.

—Dr. Lynn N. Hershey

MAHN-GO-TAH-SEE MESS

1 pound hamburger
1 cup mushroom soup
1½ cups minute rice (cooked)
⅓ cup cheese, cut up
Milk
Onion (small)
Salt
Pepper

Salt and pepper hamburger to taste. Brown chopped onion and hamburger. Cook minute rice and add to meat. In another pan heat mushroom soup, one-half soup can of milk and cheese. Serve over the meat and rice.

This is a favorite from camp. My boys named it.

—Mrs. Calvert Thomas

GREEN NOODLES AL PESTO

1 pound green noodles or spaghetti (green noodles contain spinach)
5 cloves garlic, chopped
¾ cup olive oil
½ cup Parmesan cheese
3 tablespoons fresh basil leaves, chopped. Dry will do.
½ cup chopped English walnuts
Salt
Pepper

Cook noodles in salted water. Mix remaining ingredients together. When noodles are ready toss in the mixture. Serve with more Parmesan cheese and Italian bread. My children like this very much.

—Mrs. Laurence Barker

PORK CHOP CASSEROLE

6 medium thick pork chops
1 large onion
2 green peppers
¼ cup pimento (optional)
1½ cups raw rice
1 can consommé
1 can cream of mushroom soup
1 teaspoon salt
½ - ¾ cup water

Brown chops in skillet. In bottom of casserole combine rice, pimento, ½ cup chopped green pepper, ½ cup chopped onion. Place pork chops on these. On each pork chop place thin slice of onion and green pepper. Combine consommé, mushroom soup and water and pour over all. Bake at 350° for 1 hour. Serves 6.

—Mrs. G. Bretnell Williams

POTATO CHIP CASSEROLE

2 cans chunk tuna fish
3 cups white sauce
3 cups potato chips, broken
1 can mushroom soup
1 cup carrots
1 cup peas

Mix all ingredients together, except potato chips. Place half of mixture in casserole; then layer of potato chips. Repeat. Bake for 45 minutes at 350°. Serves 8 to 10.

—**Mrs. Flora Leslie**

CONFETTI RICE

- 1 cup cooked rice
- 1/2 cup butter
- 3 eggs, slightly beaten
- 1 20-ounce can bean sprouts, drained
- 1/2 cup chopped fresh green onion tops
- 1/2 cup chopped green onion bottoms
- 5 tablespoons cut pimento strips
- 1 teaspoon salt
- 1/8 teaspoon pepper

Melt butter in large skillet. Scramble eggs with or without milk as desired until moist but set.

Add rice and remaining ingredients. Mix well. Cover and cook slowly for 10 minutes. If dry, add 2 tablespoons butter.

This may be dressed up for company by packing in a greased six cup ring mold which has been heated. Turn out on platter.

—Mrs. Philip E. Lachman

SPAGHETTI CREOLE

- 1 pound spaghetti
- 1 1/2 pounds ground beef
- 1 large yellow onion, chopped fine
- 1 large green pepper, chopped fine
- 2 cups tomatoes
- 1 can tomato soup
- 1 tablespoon sugar
- 1 teaspoon salt
- 1 1/2 teaspoons oregano

Sauté onion with green pepper and ground beef. Add tomatoes, tomato soup, sugar, salt and oregano. Add to cooked and drained spaghetti. Pour into casserole and bake for 30 minutes at 350°.

—Mrs. Flora Leslie

MY FAVORITE SPAGHETTI—(With Hot Dogs)

- 2 tablespoons shortening
- 2 tablespoons flour
- 1 bouillon cube dissolved in 1 cup boiling water
- 1 can tomato soup
- 1 tablespoon minced onion
- 1/2 teaspoon salt
- 1/4 cup sweet pickle relish
- 1 teaspoon Worcestershire sauce
- Hot dogs or cooked ground beef
- Spaghetti, cooked

Melt shortening. Stir in flour. Add mixture of bouillon, water, tomato soup, onion and salt. Simmer until thick and add pickle relish and Worcestershire sauce. Add hot dogs or ground beef. Pour over spaghetti and bake for 35 minutes at 350°.

—Mrs. Wallace T. Cripps

OREGANO SPAGHETTI SAUCE AND MEAT BALLS

- 1/4 cup chopped onion
- 1 tablespoon dried parsley flakes
- 1/2 cup chopped celery
- 2 tablespoons olive oil
- 1/8 teaspoon garlic powder
- 2 tablespoons tomato paste
- 1 bay leaf
- 1 teaspoon oregano
- 1/4 teaspoon salt
- 1/8 teaspoon black pepper
- 2 cups canned tomatoes
- 1 cup water
- 1 beef bouillon cube
- 1 cup fresh thinly sliced mushrooms
- 1/4 cup Parmesan cheese, grated (optional)

Fry onions, parsley flakes and celery in olive oil until tender. Add all remaining ingredients and simmer for one hour. Serve with meat balls over long, thin spaghetti. Garnish with cheese, if desired. Serves 4.

MEAT BALLS

- 1/2 pound ground beef
- 2 slices bread
- 1/4 cup milk
- 1 egg
- 1 small onion, chopped
- 2 tablespoons butter
- 1/4 teaspoon oregano
- 1/2 teaspoon salt
- 1/4 teaspoon pepper
- 1/4 cup Parmesan cheese, grated
- Flour

Mix meat with bread that has been soaked in milk, wrung dry and broken into small bits. Add milk and egg. Sauté onion in butter until tender; add with seasonings to meat mixture. Stir in cheese. Form into small balls and roll in flour. Brown in butter in which onions were fried until slightly browned. Drop into boiling spaghetti sauce and simmer one-half hour. Serves 4.

—Mrs. David G. Booth

SPANISH RICE

- 1 large yellow onion, chopped fine
- 1 large green pepper, chopped fine

Sauté in pan and add to:

- 3 cups cooked rice
- 1 can tomato soup
- 1 1/2 cups cooked tomatoes
- 1 1/2 pounds ground beef
- 1 teaspoon salt
- 1/4 teaspoon black pepper

Pour into baking pan or casserole and bake for 30 minutes at 350° until brown. This also can be made with lean bacon. Makes 2 quart casserole. Serves 8 to 10.

—Mrs. Flora Leslie

SUKIYAKI
(Japanese Dish)

6 cubes beef bouillon	1 10-ounce can bamboo shoots, sliced
2 cups water	
1/2 cup soy sauce	1 15-ounce can mushroom slices
Sugar to taste	1 pound 2 ounce can yam noodles
3 large sweet onions, sliced thinly	2 pounds fillet of beef, sliced paper thin
2 bunches scallions, chopped fine	4 cups cooked rice

In hot iron or electric skillet make a sauce of bouillon cubes, water, soy sauce and sugar. Add onions to sauce, they take longer to cook. When onions are almost cooked add scallions, bamboo shoots, mushrooms and noodles. Cook in separate sections of skillet. Do not mix. Finally add meat, it cooks rapidly. Serve each person a bowl of hot rice. As ingredients cook place separately in bowl of rice. Sukiyaki is a continuous process of cooking and serving. Serves 6. Very delicious!

Fun to sit on pillows on floor and eat with chop sticks, a native custom of the Japanese. Can be served with favorite green salad and sherbet or mandarin oranges. Tea, of course!

—Mrs. Leonard Meldman

TROPICAL TREAT

2 - 3 pounds lean shoulder pork, cut in small squares	1/2 cup brown sugar
	1 teaspoon salt
2 - 3 pounds white meat of chicken, cubed	1/2 cup vinegar
	2 tablespoons soy sauce
1/2 cup cooking oil	2 cups pineapple juice
1/2 cup water	1 cup chopped green peppers
4 tablespoons corn flour (any flour will do)	1/2 cup onions, thinly sliced
	2 - 3 cups pineapple chunks

Brown meat in oil. Add water, cover and cook on low fire for about 1 hour. (May be done hours before dinner.) Combine flour, sugar, salt, vinegar, soy sauce and pineapple juice and cook over low heat, stirring constantly until slightly thickened. Pour sauce over hot meat. Let stand 10 minutes. Add cooked peppers and onions and pineapple chunks. Heat altogether for about 5 minutes. Serve separately over hot rice. Serves 8.

—Mrs. E. Steven Bauer

SHRIMP A LA CREOLE

1 pound sharp Frankenmuth cheese
½ pint coffee cream
1 can Italian tomato paste
2 pounds shrimp

Cut up cheese in small pieces and melt in double boiler. Stir in coffee cream until smooth, add tomato paste. When this is well blended add shrimp until thoroughly heated. Serve over rice garnished with water cress. Serves 4.

—Mrs. Ralph L. Polk, Jr.

WILD RICE AND SHELLFISH CASSEROLE

½ pound butter
½ pound cooked crab meat
½ pound cooked shrimp
½ pound fresh mushrooms, cut in pieces
1 small green pepper, chopped fine
½ cup cooked white rice
½ cup cooked wild rice
½ cup chopped celery
1 onion, cut fine
Salt
Pepper
Few drops Tabasco sauce
2 cups heavy cream
½ cup toasted bread crumbs, buttered
⅓ cup blanched slivered almonds
2 tablespoons flour
1 cup milk, hot
2 tablespoons chopped parsley

Set oven at 400°. Melt 6 tablespoons butter in frying pan and sauté onions, celery, green pepper and mushrooms until they begin to brown, about 5 minutes. Remove from heat; add white rice and stir lightly with fork. Add this to wild rice and then add shrimp and crab meat. Mix lightly and add salt, pepper and Tabasco sauce to taste. Transfer to well buttered 2 quart casserole and pour over all 1 cup cream. Melt 2 tablespoons butter in small sauce pan and add bread crumbs and stir over low heat until crumbs are well buttered. Sprinkle over casserole. Dot with 4 tablespoons butter, cover and bake for 30 minutes at 400°. Remove cover last 10 minutes to brown on top. In the meantime sauté slivered almonds in 2 tablespoons butter until lightly browned. Make a medium thick cream sauce using 2 tablespoons butter, 2 tablespoons flour and milk. Season to taste with salt and stir in 1 cup heavy cream. Keep hot over boiling water. Serve casserole sprinkled with chopped parsley and accompanied by the cream sauce and toasted almonds. Serves 6 to 8. This is a wonderful party dish.

—Mrs. James H. Carmel

YORKSHIRE BURGERS

1½ pounds ground beef
1 package large onion soup mix
2 tablespoons chopped parsley
¼ teaspoon pepper
¼ teaspoon poultry seasoning
¼ cup chili sauce
1 tablespoon water

1½ cups flour
1½ teaspoons baking powder
1 teaspoon salt
5 eggs
1½ cups milk
3 tablespoons melted butter

Combine ground beef, soup mix, parsley, pepper, poultry seasoning and chili sauce. Blend 1 slightly beaten egg with water and add to meat mixture. Mix. Form into 24 balls. Place in well greased baking dish.

Mix and sift flour, baking powder and salt. Beat remaining eggs until foamy. Add milk and butter. Mix well. Add dry ingredients all at once to egg mixture. Beat with rotary beater or low speed mixer until smooth and well blended. Pour over meat balls. Bake at 350° for 50-60 minutes or until golden brown. This recipe by a fourteen year old boy.

—Dr. Lynn N. Hershey

OYSTER CASSEROLE

1 cup mushrooms, sliced
8 tablespoons butter, melted
1 cup bread crumbs

2 pints oysters
1 cup milk
½ cup light cream

Slice mushrooms and sauté in 2 tablespoons butter. Line bottom of greased casserole with ⅓ cup bread crumbs; add a layer of mushrooms and dot with 1 tablespoon butter. Add another layer of crumbs, then oysters and remaining sliced mushrooms and a final layer of crumbs. Pour milk, cream and remaining 5 tablespoons melted butter over top. Bake at 350° for 25 minutes. Serves 6.

—Mrs. Carleton P. McLain, Jr.

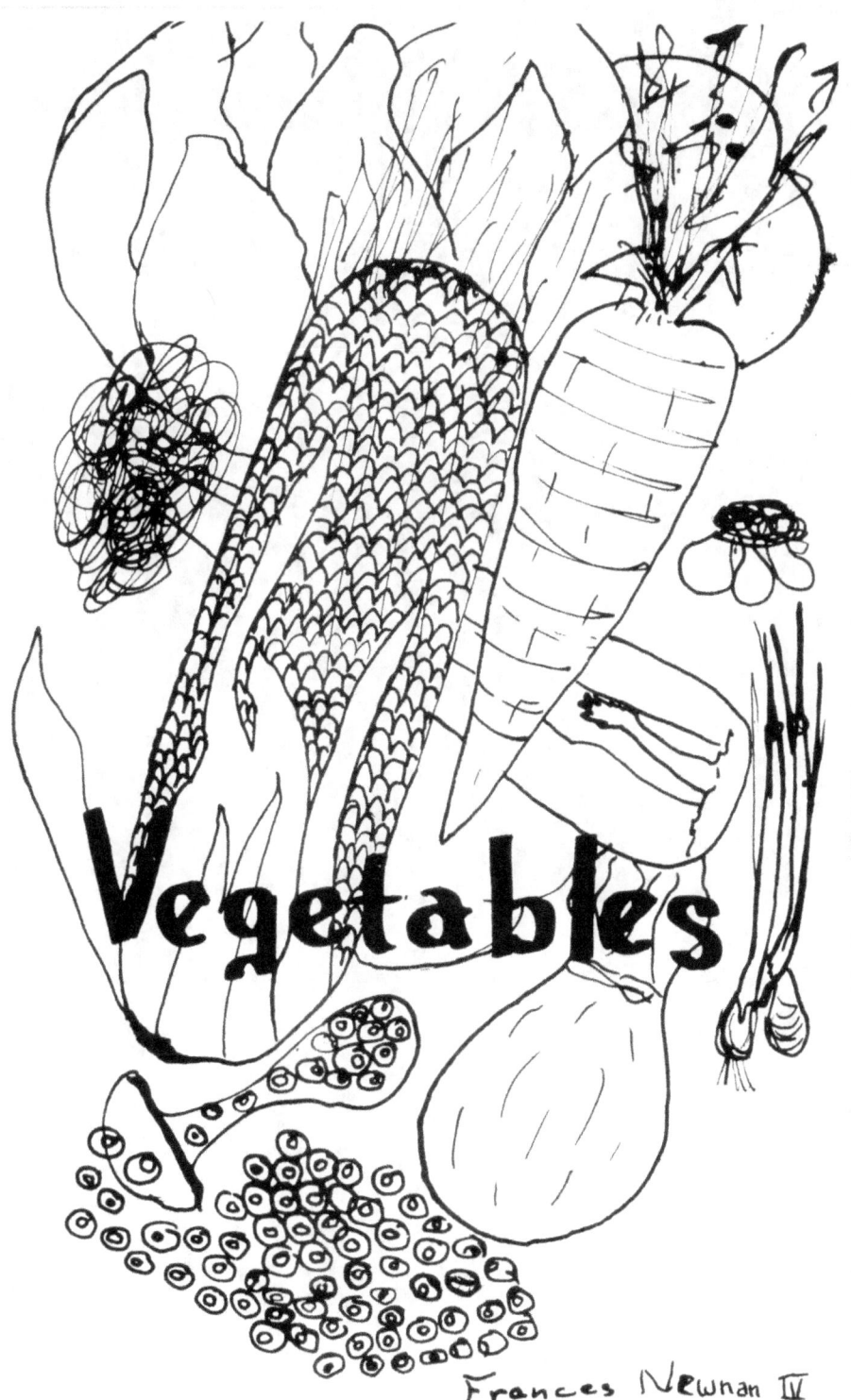

SWISS BEANS

1 pound green beans (French)
2 tablespoons butter
2 tablespoons flour
1 cup sour cream
1/2 teaspoon salt
1/8 teaspoon pepper
1 teaspoon sugar
1/2 teaspoon grated onion
1/2 pound grated Swiss cheese
paprika

Make a white sauce of butter, flour, sour cream and seasonings. Add pre-cooked green beans. Toss. Place in casserole. Top with grated cheese and paprika if desired. Bake at 375° for 20 minutes or until cheese is melted and casserole is bubbling.
—Mrs. David P. Williams

LIMA AND GREEN BEAN CASSEROLE

3 packages baby lima beans
2 packages French-cut green beans
Dash baking soda

Cook separately to slightly under-done point. Add dash baking soda to retain green color.

Cream Sauce

1/2 cup butter
6 tablespoons flour
3 teaspoons salt
1/2 teaspoon black pepper
4 dashes red pepper
1/2 teaspoon Worcestershire sauce
1 1/2 cups milk
1/2 cup cream

Topping

1/4 cup butter, diced
1 cup Parmesan cheese

Mix beans and cream sauce in large casserole dish. Top with butter and Parmesan cheese and bake in medium oven until brown. This can be made and refrigerated the day before. Heat through before topping is added. Serves 12.
—Mrs. Robert L. Martin

CAULIFLOWER AND TOMATO CASSEROLE

Cauliflower flowerets
Butter
Bread crumbs
Parmesan cheese, grated
Sliced tomatoes, or drained canned tomatoes may be used
Salt
Pepper

Parboil cauliflower flowerets. Butter a casserole and place on the bottom a layer of cauliflower. Dot with pieces of butter and sprinkle with bread crumbs; then cover with Parmesan cheese. Next place a layer of sliced tomatoes. Season with salt and pepper. Repeat this until the dish is full. Bake for 1 hour at 300°. Serves 6.
—Mrs. William L. Mitchell

BAKED BEANS

3 16-ounce cans pork and beans
1 cup chopped onion
1/2 cup chopped green pepper
2 cloves garlic, chopped fine
1/2 pound fried, diced bacon
1/4 pound salt pork, cubed
1/2 cup catsup
1/2 cup dark brown sugar
1 1/2 teaspoons dry mustard
No other seasoning

Simmer salt pork until tender (2 to 3 hours). Drain off salty and greasy fluid. Drain beans. Mix together beans, onions, green pepper, garlic, bacon and salt pork. Mix brown sugar and mustard in separate bowl. Place 1/2 bean mixture in greased baking dish. Sprinkle 1/3 sugar-mustard mixture on top. Add remainder of bean mixture and then rest of sugar mixture. Top dish with catsup, spreading evenly.
Do not overfill casserole, because when covered juice may boil out. Bake at 275° (cold oven) for 2 1/2 hours. Cover casserole for first 2 hours. Uncover last 1/2 hour. Serves 10 to 12.
—Dr. Lynn N. Hershey

EGGPLANT CASSEROLE

1 large eggplant
7 tiny tender green zucchini squash
2 cups rich homemade chicken stock
8 saltine crackers, crushed fine
1 cup sharp cheese, grated
Many dabs of butter
Black pepper

Dice eggplant (medium sized pieces) and zucchini. Leave skin on after washing and cut into thin slices. Sauté eggplant and zucchini squash with butter and some chicken broth in large skillet till tender. Put into casserole, add saltine crackers crushed, add cheese and butter throughout and remaining chicken broth. Bake for 45 minutes. Season with black pepper. Serves 16.
—Mrs. G. Bretnell Williams

GREEN BEAN CASSEROLE

2 packages frozen French-cut green beans
2 cans mushroom soup
1 can French fried onions

Cook beans 5 minutes in boiling salted water. Drain well and add mushroom soup. Place in casserole and heat 1/2 hour at 350°. Remove from oven and sprinkle top with onions. Return to oven for 15 minutes. If the children hate green vegetables, they'll eat the onions. You can't lose.
—Mrs. Alfred C. Moore

CUCUMBERS IN CHEESE

2 cucumbers   3 medium slices American cheese
Cream sauce

Peel cucumbers, split lengthwise and remove seeds. Cut in cubes and cook about 15 or 20 minutes. Drain thoroughly. Make a cream sauce as you usually do and when finished add slices of cheese. Melt them in the sauce. Add cucumbers and heat through thoroughly. Strangely enough, our boys love them.

—Mrs. Alfred C. Moore

ITALIAN EGGPLANT

1 eggplant	1 onion
1 large can tomatoes	Grated yellow cheese
1 small can tomato purée	4 slices yellow cheese
1 green pepper	

Peel and slice eggplant. Brown the slices a little in hot butter in a frying pan. Chop onion and green pepper and sauté in a pan Add tomatoes and the tomato purée for thickening. Place a layer of eggplant in the bottom of a buttered casserole. Pour over some of the sauce, then the grated cheese. Repeat until the casserole is filled. Top with a layer of sliced, processed yellow cheese. Bake slowly about 1/2 hour. Serves 6.

—Mrs. William L. Mitchell

LIMA BEAN POT

1 pound large dried lima beans	1/3 cup diced celery
8 cups water	1 tablespoon brown sugar
2 pounds or more boneless smoked pork butts	1 teaspoon dry mustard
2 onions, chopped	1/2 teaspoon salt

Pick over beans. Add 6 cups water and bring to boil. Boil 2 minutes. Let stand 1 hour. Put beans on to cook with pork butts, add 2 more cups water, onions, celery, brown sugar, mustard and salt. Cover and simmer 2 1/2 hours. Slice meat and serve over beans. Sprinkle with parsley. Serves 4 to 6.

—Mrs. Robert G. Wild

MUSHROOMS IN SOUR CREAM

1/2 cup butter	2 tablespoons flour
4 tablespoons chopped challots	1 1/2 cups sour cream
2 pounds button mushrooms, washed	Dash of sherry wine
	Salt and pepper

Brown challots lightly in melted butter. Add mushrooms and cook 5 minutes. Stir in flour and cook 3 minutes more. Add sour cream, sherry, and salt and pepper to taste. Heat through and serve on triangles of toast. Serves 8.

—Mrs. Calvert Thomas

POTATO PIE

2 eggs	1 teaspoon salt
Pinch baking powder	2 tablespoons flour
2 cups raw grated potatoes	3 tablespoons shortening

Beat eggs. Add the other ingredients, except shortening. Mix together. Pour the melted shortening into a pie pan and pour in mixture. Bake about 1 hour at 400°. Serve with meat or chicken. Serves 6.

—Mrs. Charles S. Himelhoch

WILD RICE

1 1/2 cups washed raw wild rice	3 heaping tablespoons celery and leaves (mostly leaves)
1/4 pound butter	4 cups undiluted broth or consommé
3 heaping tablespoons chopped onion	

Melt butter over direct heat. Add wild rice, onions and celery. Sauté for a few minutes; then cover and simmer until onions look transparent. Add broth or consommé. Cook covered until rice gets soft and liquid almost disappears. Takes at least 1 1/2 hours. If served with chicken, use chicken broth.

—Mrs. Clifford B. West

BIGOS
(Sauerkraut Polish style)

1 can sauerkraut	1 teaspoon salt
1 can tomatoes	Pepper
1 pound Polish sausage, cut in pieces	Bay leaf
1 onion	Carrot, if desired

Combine all ingredients together. Bring to boil and simmer for 1 hour.

—Mrs. Gustaw Konopnicki

SQUASH ROCKEFELLER
(A Louisiana Dish)

6 small yellow summer squash
1 package spinach, frozen
Onions
Salt
Pepper
Oregano
2 tablespoons anisette
Buttered bread crumbs
Dash Parmesan cheese

Parboil squash. Slice in halves and scoop out seeds. To the spinach add onions which have been sautéed in butter. Cook lightly. Add salt, pepper, a little oregano and anisette. Fill squash with the spinach mixture; cover with buttered bread crumbs and Parmesan cheese and bake until squash is tender.

—Mrs. Richard K. Scales

SPINACH SOUFFLE

3 packages frozen chopped spinach
1 tablespoon dried mushrooms
2 cans cream of mushroom soup, undiluted
1 tablespoon butter
1 onion, minced
3 eggs, separated
Salt
Pepper

Sauté minced onion and mushrooms in butter. Add soup, egg yolks, salt and pepper. Cook for 10 minutes over slow heat. Beat egg whites. Boil spinach 1 minute and drain well. Add to mushroom sauce. Fold in stiff egg whites. Put in uncovered casserole and bake at 350° for 50 - 60 minutes. Serves 8 to 10.

—Mrs. Carleton P. McLain, Jr.

TURNIP FLUFF

2 pounds turnips, pared and cubed
1/4 cup light cream
1 egg, beaten
2 tablespoons butter, melted
1/4 cup light brown sugar
2 tablespoons uncooked cream of wheat
Salt and pepper to taste

Cook turnips in 1 inch boiling salted water until tender. Drain thoroughly. Mash. Add remaining ingredients. Blend well. Pile lightly in greased 1 quart casserole. Bake at 350° for 40 minutes. Serves 6.

—Mrs. Robert G. Wild

TOMATOES STUFFED WITH GRILLED MUSHROOMS

6 medium size tomatoes
1 pound mushrooms
Lemon juice
1/4 pound butter
1/2 cup canned tomato sauce
1 egg yolk
Salt
Black peppercorns
Basil
Buttered bread crumbs

Wash and dry mushooms and cut them into small pieces. Sprinkle with lemon juice and cook in butter in iron skillet over high heat until they are dry. Shake pan and stir while they cook. Remove from heat. Add tomato sauce which has been mixed with egg yolk. Season to taste with salt, pepper and basil. Scoop out tomatoes and stuff with mushroom mixture. Sprinkle with buttered bread crumbs.

—Mrs. E. Steven Bauer

BAKED CHICKEN WITH DRESSING

1 large stewing hen	1 large onion
3 stalks celery	1 teaspoon salt

Simmer chicken covered until tender. When cool remove chicken from bones. Keep in large pieces. Grease baking dish. Put a layer of dressing and a layer of chicken. Repeat.

Dressing

1 loaf day old bread	1 teaspoon salt (scant)
1 cup butter	1 teaspoon poultry seasoning
1 cup celery, chopped	1 teaspoon sage
1 cup onion, chopped	1/2 teaspoon accent salt

Remove crust from bread and cut in cubes. Sauté celery, onion and salt in melted butter. Add bread cubes, poultry seasoning, sage and accent salt. Thicken stock from chicken and pour over the layers of chicken and dressing. Bake for 45 minutes at 325° until golden brown. Serves 8 to 10.

—Mrs. Flora Leslie

BAKED CHICKEN

2 fryers, disjointed	1 can cream of mushroom soup
3/4 cup raw white rice	1/2 soup can milk
1 pound sliced fresh or canned drained mushrooms (optional)	1 package dried onion soup mix
	Paprika

Spread rice in a thin layer over bottom of a large shallow baking pan. If mushrooms are used lay them on top of rice. Cover with single layer of chicken. Sprinkle onion soup mix over chicken. Blend milk with cream of mushroom soup and pour over layers of rice and chicken. Sprinkle with paprika. Bake uncovered for 1 - 1 1/2 hours at 325°. If it seems to be drying out add a little extra milk and cover with aluminum foil. To reheat: add a little milk, cover and heat slowly in oven at 325°. This can be made a day ahead and cooked just before serving or may be baked and frozen for reheating at a later date.

—Mrs. Peter Kerr

BEEF STROGANOFF (Easy)

2 - 3 pounds beef, cut into bite size pieces	1 tablespoon soy sauce
Flour seasoned with salt	1 tablespoon Worcestershire sauce
$1\frac{1}{3}$ cups water	$\frac{1}{4}$ cup catsup or tomato sauce
1 package dried onion soup mix	$\frac{1}{4}$ cup sherry
	2 - 3 tablespoons sour cream

Coat pieces of meat with flour and salt. In hot fat in Dutch oven or heavy skillet brown meat slowly. Add water and onion soup mix. Bring to boil and let simmer for 1 - 2 hours or until meat is tender. Add catsup, Worcestershire sauce and soy sauce. Just before serving add sherry and sour cream. Heat but do not boil. Serve over noodles or rice.

—Mrs. Robert L. Martin

CHOP SUEY

1 pound chopped beef	1 teaspoon salt
1 pound chopped lean pork	$\frac{1}{4}$ teaspoon pepper

Roll above ingredients in $\frac{1}{2}$ cup flour and sauté; add 2 cups of water and cook until tender.

Cook:

$1\frac{1}{2}$ cups celery, cut in 1 inch pieces	1 cup onions, cut in 1 inch pieces

Cook only until tender. When meat is cooked add the following vegetables and liquids:

1 No. 2 can bean sprouts	2 tablespoons Kitchen Bouquet
1 6-ounce can mushrooms	$\frac{1}{4}$ cup molasses
1 tablespoon soy sauce	$\frac{1}{4}$ cup cornstarch

Cook altogether for 15 minutes and serve on buttered rice or chow mein noodles. This will freeze well. Serves 8 to 10.

—Mrs. Flora Leslie

DUCK, VENISON, ELK

Sprinkle inside cavity with salt, pepper and oregano. Place inside cavity:

1 carrot	1 piece celery
1 small onion	

Melt $\frac{1}{2}$ stick margarine in 2 cups dry sherry (for 2 ducks). Pour hot mixture over duck in roasting pan. Cover. Cook for 3 hours at 300°. Turn duck breast up $\frac{1}{2}$ hour before end of cooking. Best ever! Good with tame duck.

—Dr. Lynn N. Hershey

FRENCH ROAST DUCK WITH WINE SAUCE

Have butcher quarter 1 frozen duck. Roast uncovered at 325° for 2 hours.

Wine Sauce

2 tablespoons butter	1 cup currant jelly
2 tablespoons flour	1 cup wine
1 cup boiling water	2 oranges

Brown flour with butter in sauce pan. Add water, stir until smooth, add currant jelly and blend well; cook for 5 minutes. Add wine and remove from heat. Peel, section and remove outer skin of oranges and drop into sauce. Pour over duck and reduce oven to 200°. Bake for 1 more hour in covered roaster.
—Mrs. Leonard Meldman

HAM LOAF

2½ pounds smoked ham, ground	1 teaspoon grated onion
½ pound ground veal	1½ cups milk
3 eggs	½ teaspoon pepper

Mix and pour into greased loaf pan. Put on topping.

Topping

½ cup brown sugar	1 teaspoon dry mustard
1 teaspoon cloves	

Mix together and spread over top of loaf. Bake at 325° for 1 hour and 15 minutes. Serves 8 to 10. —Mrs. Flora Leslie

PINEAPPLE HAM LOAF

1½ pounds ham, ground with	1 cup bread crumbs
½ pound pork	½ teaspoon celery salt
1 tablespoon butter	¼ teaspoon black pepper
½ cup brown sugar	2 eggs, beaten
6 slices pineapple	2 tablespoons baking powder
⅓ cup chopped green pepper	1 cup milk
3 tablespoons chopped onion	

Mix the butter and brown sugar together and pat it evenly in the bottom of a loaf pan. Place the slices of pineapple in a layer over the butter and sugar mixture. In a large bowl mix the ground meat, green pepper, onion, bread crumbs, celery salt, pepper, eggs, baking powder and milk. Mix this all together thoroughly and pat the mixture over the pineapple slices. Bake for 1 hour and twenty minutes at 375°. Turn out on a platter just like an upside down cake. —Mrs. William L. Mitchell

HAMBURGERS

2 pounds ground beef or ground steak
2 eggs
1 cup bread crumbs
2 teaspoons salt
1/4 cup chopped onion
1/2 teaspoon black pepper
1/2 cup milk

Shape into patties. Bake at 400° for 15 minutes or until brown. Serves 8 to 10.

—Mrs. Flora Leslie

HAWAIIAN CURRY

2 cups coconut milk
1/2 cup minced onion
1/3 cup butter
1 tablespoon curry
1 teaspoon salt
1/4 teaspoon ginger
2 cups chicken broth
3 cups diced, cooked chicken
1 1/2 cups canned pineapple chunks

Cook onion in butter until soft, not brown. Blend in flour. Add curry, salt, ginger, coconut milk and chicken broth. Cook over low heat, stirring constantly until thickened. Add chicken and pineapple. Heat thoroughly.
Serve with fluffy rice and chutney. Serves 6.
Suggestion: best to use canned, concentrated coconut powder.

—Mrs. William L. Mitchell

KOFTAS
(An Indian recipe)

3 - 4 pounds ground lamb
2 eggs
2 - 3 medium sized onions, chopped
1 teaspoon ginger, ground
1 clove garlic (I leave this out, but some like it)
Mint and coriander leaves
3 - 4 tomatoes, cut up or 1 large can stewed tomatoes
2 - 3 tablespoons curry
Oil
Salt
Pepper
Water

Add salt and eggs to meat and make small balls, 1 - 2 inches in diameter. Pour a little oil into a pot and fry onions until light brown. Add ginger, garlic and paste of curry powder and water and fry until onions are mashed and curry gives an aroma. Add water, tomatoes, mint, coriander, salt and meat balls. Let simmer for about 1/2 hour until the sauce thickens and meat balls are cooked. Serve hot with rice. Serves 8.

—Mrs. E. Steven Bauer

HUNGARIAN POT ROAST

4 pounds boned beef rump roast
¼ cup flour
2 tablespoons fat
4 teaspoons salt
2 medium onions, quartered
1 teaspoon caraway seed
½ teaspoon pepper
1½ cups tomato juice

Dredge meat with flour and brown on all sides in hot fat. Add salt, onions, caraway seed, pepper and tomato juice. Cover and cook over low heat on top of range or in a moderate oven 350° for about 3½ hours. Add water if necessary.
Serve with hot buttered noodles. Serves 6 to 8.

—Mrs. William F. Thomas

SWISS LIVER AND ONIONS

2 medium onions, sliced
¼ cup melted butter or margarine
1½ pounds beef liver, cut in 1 inch strips
1½ teaspoons salt
Dash pepper
4 ounce can mushrooms, undrained
2 tablespoons flour
1 cup commercial sour cream
½ teaspoon Worcestershire sauce

Cook onions in melted butter in skillet until tender, stirring occasionally. Add liver; brown lightly on both sides. Season with salt and pepper; add mushrooms and liquid. Cover and simmer for 15 minutes or until tender. Remove liver and onions from skillet. Blend together flour and sour cream. Add ¼ cup gravy from skillet; stir until smooth. Pour gradually into skillet. Mix well. Heat over low heat, stirring constantly until thickened. Stir in Worcestershire sauce. Add liver and onions and heat. Serves 6. My favorite liver recipe.

—Mrs. Leonard Latos

SALMON LOAF

1 pound can salmon
1½ cups soft bread crumbs
1 cup milk plus liquid from salmon
3 eggs, slightly beaten
½ cup onion, chopped
½ cup butter, melted
1 teaspoon salt
1 teaspoon pepper
1 tablespoon Worcestershire sauce

Drain salmon and reserve liquid. Remove bones and skin from salmon and break into pieces. Sauté onions in butter until tender. Add crumbs, milk and liquid, eggs and seasonings. Mix altogether and bake at 350° for 1 hour. Serves 8 to 10.

—Mrs. Flora Leslie

SWEET-SOUR MEAT BALLS

2 pounds ground round steak (ground twice)
2 eggs
1 large grated onion
3 tablespoons catsup
½ cup bread crumbs
Salt, and freshly ground pepper
Garlic salt

Mix all ingredients lightly and roll into small balls. Melt ¼ pound of butter in a skillet and brown the meat balls in the butter. Remove from skillet.

Sauce

2 cups water
½ cup dark brown sugar
⅛ cup lemon juice
10 ginger snaps
½ cup white raisins
1 medium sized cabbage

Bring the water to a boil. Add brown sugar, lemon juice, ginger snaps and raisins. Stir well and continue cooking about five minutes. Shred the cabbage into medium sized strips and stir it into the sauce mixture. Place the meat balls in a casserole, cover with sauce and bake for 3 hours at 350°.

—Mrs. William L. Mitchell

SWEET AND SOUR PORK

2 large green bell peppers
¾ cup shortening
1 teaspoon salt
1 clove garlic
2 eggs
4 teaspoons flour
1 teaspoon salt
1/16 teaspoon pepper
1 pound lean pork
2 cups chicken bouillon
1 small can pineapple tidbits
3 teaspoons cornstarch
2 teaspoons soy sauce
⅓ cup vinegar
½ cup sugar

Cut peppers into 12 pieces each. Cook in boiling water for 8 minutes. Heat shortening with 1 teaspoon salt and chopped garlic. Make batter of eggs, flour, salt and pepper. Cut pork into 1 inch cubes and dip in batter. Brown in hot grease on all all sides. Remove pieces as they brown. Drain off all but 1 tablespoon grease. Add 1 cup bouillon, pineapple and its juice, peppers and pork. Cover tightly and simmer for 10 minutes. Blend together cornstarch, soy sauce, vinegar, sugar and 1 cup bouillon. Add to pork mixture, stirring constantly until juice thickens and mixture is very hot. Serve over rice or chow mein noodles. May be made ahead and reheated. Serves 4.

—Mrs. David E. Barney

MILANESAS

10 thin slices boneless chuck roast, easy to slice when half frozen
3 eggs
2 teaspoons grated onion
3 tablespoons chopped parsley
1 teaspoon chopped garlic
Salt
Pepper
Breadcrumbs, dry
Lemon slices

Beat the eggs. Add parsley, onion, garlic, salt and pepper. Dip pieces of meat one by one into this mixture; then roll in breadcrumbs pressing them with your hands. Fry in oil or fat that is not too hot until golden brown. Do not fry too dark or they will be dry. Serve with slices of lemon and potato salad or mashed potatoes. —Mrs. Laurence Barker

FOOLPROOF SOUFFLE
(For Main Dish or Dessert)

1 teaspoon butter
1/2 cup soft bread crumbs
3 egg yolks
1/4 teaspoon salt
1 cup milk
3 egg whites, beaten stiff

Mix and cook all ingredients, except egg whites, for 3 minutes; fold in egg whites. Fill individual souffle dishes or one baking dish and bake in moderate oven for 15 minutes. This dish will not fall and can be left in oven, turned off, for a short while. Serves 4.

For other main dish variations add before baking: 1 cup grated cheese or 1 cup cut up ham and serve with fruit salad.
For dessert, add before baking: melted chocolate and 1 cup sugar or sugar and raisins and 1 teaspoon vanilla.
—Mrs. Francis C. McMath

BAKED VEAL CHOPS WITH CURRY SAUCE

6 veal chops
3 tablespoons butter
1 teaspoon onion, chopped
1/2 cup celery, chopped
1 grated apple
2 teaspoons flour
1 1/2 cups chicken broth
1 teaspoon curry
Dash ginger
Dash paprika
1/2 cup cream
2 teaspoons chopped parsley

Brown veal chops in butter. Remove from pan. Add all ingredients in order listed to remaining butter in pan. Return meat to pan. Bake covered for 20 minutes at 400°. Remove cover. Bake for 10 more minutes. —Mrs. David P. Williams

FLANK STEAK

1½ pounds flank steak
Salt, pepper, ginger
Pitted cooked prunes and syrup
Apples, peeled and sliced
2 cups beef bouillon or consommé
Tart jelly (optional)

Rub steak on both sides with salt, pepper and ginger. Arrange prunes and apples on top. Fold over and tie with string or fasten with skewers. Sear in butter on all sides until brown. Add liquid. (Syrup from the cooked prunes, consommé. Some tart jelly may also be added.) Bake in a moderate oven 350°, basting occasionally, until meat is tender, usually about 2 hours. Make a gravy from the liquid in the pan.

—Mrs. Clifford B. West

INDIVIDUAL TURKEY PIES
Crust

3 cups flour
1 teaspoon salt
½ cup lard
3 tablespoons butter
¼ cup cold water

Roll out pie crust and cut with a round cutter (6 inch).

Filling

3 cups turkey, cut in bite size pieces)
Turkey gravy

Moisten turkey with gravy. Place ¼ cup of meat in center of pastry. Fold over and press ends together. Prick with fork. Bake for 20 minutes at 400°. Serves 8 to 10.

—Mrs. Flora Leslie

TARRAGON VEAL

1 pound veal steak
½ - ¾ cup sauterne
1 tablespoon dried tarragon, pulverized

Sear veal on both sides in hot frying pan. Then add sauterne and tarragon. Cover tightly and simmer for 1½ hours. Add more liquid if necessary. Serves 3 to 4.

—Mrs. Alfred C. Moore

BOLOGNA BUNS

1 pound bologna	1 teaspoon prepared mustard
2 tablespoons sweet pickle, chopped	2 tablespoons salad dressing
1 tablespoon tomato catsup	Frankfurter buns

Put bologna through food chopper and add other ingredients. Fill buns and wrap in foil. Bake for 15 minutes at 350°. Serve piping hot. Serves 8.

—Mrs. Flora Leslie

SHERWOOD HOT DOGS

Hot dogs	Bacon
Cheese strips	Hot dog buns

Split hot dog lengthwise; fill with strips of cheese. Wind 1 slice of bacon around hot dog and place a tooth pick at each end. Place under broiler until cheese is melted and bacon becomes slightly browned. Watch carefully. Remove tooth picks before placing in warm bun. Serve with favorite relish.

—Mrs. Leonard Meldman

OPEN FACE SANDWICH
A La Fritz Hershey's Grandmother, Mrs. Arthur D. Spencer

1 Holland rusk or thick dried toast per serving.	½ tomato, fried in bacon fat
Grated yellow cheese, mixed with butter to form a spreading paste. Worcestershire sauce to taste, salt and pepper.	3 sardines, skinless and boneless
	Hollandaise sauce, your own favorite recipe or easy version.
	2 strips of bacon, cooked

Fix cheese on rusk or toast and fry tomatoes ahead of time. Put rusk with cheese, tomato and sardines in 400° oven while preparing Hollandaise sauce. Pour sauce over rusks and top with 2 cooked strips of bacon, crossed. This recipe for one serving. Multiply by number to be served. Very, very, Yum, Yum!

—Mrs. Spencer R. Hershey

TOASTED CHEESE SANDWICHES

1½ pounds sharp cheese
½ cup soft butter
¼ cup milk

Put cheese through grinder and mix with butter and milk until soft enough to spread. Bake for 10 minutes at 400° or until golden brown. Serves 8 to 10.

—Mrs. Flora Leslie

PIZZA
(Brookside Style)

1 pound sausage meat
1 pound ground beef
1 teaspoon salt
1 teaspoon sage
2 tablespoons minced onion
1 tablespoon oregano

Brown all ingredients. Drain off fat.

12 English muffins, cut in half
2 cups tomato sauce
¾ pound Mozzarella cheese, shredded
One inch sausage ring, mildly seasoned
Parmesan cheese
Parsley flakes

Spread English muffin halves with tomato sauce. Spread on layer of meat and layer of Mozzarella cheese; another layer of tomato sauce; another layer of cheese. Cut three slices of sausage ring and place on each muffin. Shake Parmesan cheese and parsley flakes on top. Bake for 15 minutes at 425°. Serves 8 to 10.

—Mrs. Flora Leslie

GRILLED TUNA FISH

Tuna fish
Bread
1 slice tomato
1 slice American cheese
1 strip bacon

Drain and crumble tuna fish. Spread on top of bread slices. Add tomato, cheese and top with strip of bacon. Broil until golden brown.

—Mrs. Leonard Meldman

CRUMPETS

1 cup all purpose flour	Sift altogether and add:
4 tablespoons cornstarch	2 eggs, well beaten
2 teaspoons baking soda	1/2 cup milk
2 teaspoons cream of tartar	3 tablespoons butter, melted
4 tablespoons sugar	

Mix well and drop from tablespoon onto hot griddle. Try and keep them golden brown. Serve with strawberry or black currant jam. Makes 26 small sponge-like cakes. Excellent with tea.

—Mrs. Flora Leslie

DANISH COFFEE CAKE
(Makes 2 cakes)

4 cups flour	3/4 cup milk
1 cup lard	4 tablespoons sugar
3 egg yolks	
1 yeast cake, dissolved in 1/2 cup lukewarm water	

Mix flour and lard as for pie crust. Then mix egg yolks, yeast mixture, milk and sugar; add to flour and lard mixture. Beat well and put in refrigerator until stiff, about 2 hours.

Divide dough in half. Roll out 1/4 inch thick until piece measures 12 x 10 inches. Spread half of almond filling on top of dough. Fold sides over one inch toward middle, leaving filling exposed. Let rise for 2 hours. Bake for 30 minutes at 400°. Pastry is ready to serve. If desired thin white frosting may be dribbled over coffee cake while still warm. Apricot or strawberry preserves may be used in place of almond filling.

Almond Filling

3 egg whites, beaten stiff	1/4 cup butter, melted
1 cup sugar	1 teaspoon almond extract
2 cups nuts, finely chopped	

Mix all ingredients together.

White Frosting

3 cups powdered sugar	1/4 cup boiling water

Mix together.

—Mrs. Flora Leslie

BANANA BREAD

1 cup sugar	1 teaspoon soda
1/2 cup butter	1/4 teaspoon salt
2 eggs	2 cups flour
1/4 cup sour milk	3 mashed bananas

Mix butter and sugar; add eggs, milk and dry ingredients. Add bananas. Let stand 10 minutes before baking. Put into two greased 3 x 6 inch loaf pans. Bake at 350° for 40 - 60 minutes.
—Mrs. James C. Holmes

IRISH SODA BREAD

4 cups sifted flour	1 cup raisins
1/4 cup granulated sugar	1 1/3 cups buttermilk
1 teaspoon salt	1 egg, unbeaten
1 teaspoon double acting baking powder	1 teaspoon baking soda
1/4 cup butter	1 egg yolk, beaten

Start oven at 375° and grease 2 quart casserole. Sift flour, sugar, salt and baking powder into mixing bowl. Cut in butter with pastry blender until like coarse corn meal. Stir in raisins. Combine buttermilk, egg and soda; stir into flour mixture until just moistened. Turn dough onto lightly floured surface. Knead lightly and shape into ball. Place in casserole. With sharp knife make a 4 inch cross 1/4 inch deep in center. Brush with egg yolk. Bake about 1 hour. Cool in pan 10 minutes. Then remove to finish cooling. Cuts into 20 slices.
—Mrs. Donald S. Mann

CAT-TAIL POLLEN PANCAKES

These have been called "Sunshine Flapjacks". The time to make them is in late May or early June, when the staminate, upper portions of the cat-tail heads, are ready to shed their golden pollen.

The cat-tails are easily picked and generous amounts of pollen are obtainable in just a few of them. The pollen is shaken into a bowl or on a clean cloth. Subsitute half the flour required in any plain pancake recipe for an equal amount of the pollen.
—Mrs. Janet M. Hawksley

CORN PANCAKES

2 cups canned creamed corn
2 eggs
4 tablespoons flour
1 teaspoon baking powder
Salt to taste

Mix above ingredients and fry with butter in skillet. Makes about 14 small pancakes.

—Mrs. Charles F. Delbridge, Jr.

FRENCH PANCAKES

1½ cups all purpose flour
1 teaspoon salt
2 teaspoons baking powder
4 tablespoons confectioners sugar
4 eggs, slightly beaten
1⅓ cups milk
⅔ cup water
Currant jelly or your favorite
1 teaspoon vanilla

Sift together flour, salt, baking powder and confectioners sugar. Make a well in the sifted ingredients. Pour in liquid ingredients. Combine, mashing lumps with fork until fairly smooth. Use 10 inch round pancake griddle. Set temperature at 400°. Pour enough batter to barely cover surface of griddle by tipping very fast. When pancake starts to curl at edges turn over and bake on other side. Spread with currant jelly. Roll as you would a jelly roll and sift confectioners sugar over top. Makes ten 10 inch rolled up pancakes.

—Mr. David G. Booth

POTATO PANCAKES
(Placki Kartoflane)

1 large potato
1 egg
½ teaspoon salt
½ cup flour
Milk
Corn oil

Grate potato finely, add the rest of the ingredients using just enough milk to make into a thick batter. Heat corn oil in fry pan and drop in large spoonfuls of batter. Fry until golden brown on both sides (about 1 minute each side). Drain on paper towel. These must be served piping hot. Variations in flavors such as cheese, onion, parsley, tuna, etc. may be added to batter. Particularly good with onion sauce.

P.S.: Always stir mixture before dropping into pan.

—Mrs. Gustaw Konopnicki

SOUR CREAM PANCAKES

2 cups white bread, diced
1 tablespoon melted butter
1 teaspoon sugar
2 eggs, beaten
1/4 teaspoon baking powder
1 teaspoon baking soda
1 cup hot milk
1 teaspoon salt
1 cup flour
1 cup sour cream

Beat together bread, milk, butter, salt and sugar. Add the flour and eggs. Add sour cream and baking soda and blend well. Refrigerate overnight. Before making the pancakes add the baking powder to the batter. Make pancakes thin and in a very hot pan. Makes about 40 pancakes.

—Mrs. Charles S. Himelhoch

GRANDMA'S FRENCH TOAST

6 - 8 slices day old bread
1/2 cup milk
2 eggs, slightly beaten
1/4 teaspoon salt
Butter
Maple syrup

Mix milk, eggs and salt together. Dip bread into mixture. Fry on griddle and serve with butter and maple syrup.

—Mrs. Stephen F. Booth

BLINTZ PANCAKES

1 cup sifted flour
1 tablespoon sugar
1/2 teaspoon salt
1 cup commercial sour cream
1 cup small curd cream style cottage cheese
4 well beaten eggs
Maple or blueberry syrup
Blueberry sauce

Sift dry ingredients into bowl. Add sour cream, cottage cheese and eggs. Fold only until flour is barely moistened. Bake on a hot, lightly greased griddle. Turn cakes when bubbles on surface break. Serve with maple or blueberry syrup or blueberry sauce. Makes 16 4-inch pancakes.

Blueberry sauce

1 pound can blueberries
2 teaspoons cornstarch
1 teaspoon lemon juice

Combine blueberries and cornstarch. Cook and stir until thick and clear. Add lemon juice.

—Mrs. Stephen F. Booth

YEAST ROLLS

2 yeast cakes dissolved in:
1/2 cup luke warm water
Scald:
1 1/2 cups milk and put into large bowl. Cool and add:
4 cups flour
1/2 cup sugar

2 teaspoons salt
3 eggs, well beaten
Then add the yeast mix. Beat well and add:
3 more cups flour
1/2 cup cooking oil

Knead well and cover until double in bulk. Roll out in shape desired. Let stand until doubled again. Bake at 350° for 15 - 20 minutes. Makes 6 dozen rolls. These can be frozen.

—Mrs. Flora Leslie

YORKSHIRE PUDDING

7/8 cup flour
1/2 teaspoon salt
1/2 cup milk

2 eggs
1/2 cup water

Sift flour and salt into bowl. Make well in center, pour in milk, and stir. Add eggs, beaten fluffy, and beat into batter. Add water. Beat batter until large bubbles rise to surface. Have ready hot oven-proof dish or 10" x 10" baking pan containing about 1/4 inch of hot beef drippings or melted butter. Pour in batter. Bake pudding at 350° for 1/2 hour or until golden brown. Do not overcook. Serve at once with roast beef. Serves 6.

—Mrs. John P. Denio

ORIENTAL ALMOND COOKIES

2½ cups sifted flour
1 teaspoon soda
½ cup white sugar
¾ cup brown sugar
1 egg, slightly beaten
1 tablespoon almond extract
1 cup salad oil

Mix ingredients together. Roll dough with hand (size of walnut) and flatten on cookie sheet to ¼ inch thickness. Bake at 375°-400° for 10 - 15 minutes.

—Mrs. C. B. Sung

EMPIRE BISCUITS FOR TEA

4 cups all purpose flour
2 cups soft butter
1 cup confectioners sugar
1 teaspoon vanilla
Preserves
Plain icing
Candied cherries

Mix together until dough is soft. Roll out on floured board. Cut out small rounds and bake for 10 minutes to light yellow in color. Put two rounds together with 1 teaspoon thick preserves in the midlle. Ice top with plain icing and top with candied cherry.

—Mrs. Flora Leslie

BROWNIES

4 eggs, beaten until thick
2 cups sugar
Melt and cool:
    4 squares chocolate
    ½ cup milk
    ⅔ cup butter
1 cup sifted flour
1 teaspoon baking powder
½ teaspoon salt
1 teaspoon vanilla
1 cup broken walnuts

Blend altogether. Bake for 25 minutes at 350°. Frost with chocolate frosting.

Chocolate Frosting

3 cups confectioners sugar
¼ cup evaporated milk
2 1-ounce squares chocolate, melted
¼ cup butter, melted
1 teaspoon vanilla

Beat sugar, milk and chocolate together. Slowly add butter and vanilla.

—Mrs. Flora Leslie

APRICOT-DATE BARS
No. 1 Mixture

1 pound dried apricots, cooked or soaked
½ package pitted dates
1 cup water
1 cup sugar
1 tablespoon lemon juice
½ teaspoon vanilla

Cook in double boiler until soft and into a marmalade.

No. 2 Mixture

1½ cups flour
½ teaspoon salt
½ teaspoon soda
1 cup brown sugar
1½ cups rolled oats, uncooked
1 cup melted butter
1 cup walnuts

Put No. 2 mixture in pan about 10" x 16", saving a half cup. Put No. 1 mixture on top. Sprinkle with half cup of No. 2 mixture. Bake for 25 - 30 minutes at 350°. Cut in squares.

—Mrs. David Emerman

BROWN-EYED SUSANS

¾ cup soft butter
½ cup sugar
1 egg
1 teaspoon vanilla
¼ teaspoon salt
1¾ cups sifted flour
1 7-ounce package chocolate mint candy wafers

Cream together butter, sugar, egg, vanilla and salt. Stir in flour. Chill about 1 hour. Shape in 1 inch balls. Place 2 inches apart on ungreased cooky sheet. Flatten each by pressing a wafer in center. Bake at 400° for 8 - 10 minutes. Remove immediately from pan. Makes 4 dozen cookies.

—Mrs. Stephen F. Booth

BUTTER COOKIES

1 pound butter, room temperature
1 cup sugar
2 egg yolks, slightly beaten
2 tablespoons brandy
Rind and juice of 1 lemon
5 cups cake flour
1 teaspoon baking powder

Cream butter. Add sugar, egg yolks, lemon and brandy. Work in flour and baking powder. Can be put through cookie press or rolled and cut out. Glaze cookies with beaten egg and cream. Bake for 15 minutes at 350°. Will keep for weeks. Can be decorated with jelly and frosting, cherries, nuts or any desired decoration.

—Mrs. David Emerman

BUTTERSCOTCH BROWNIES

1 cup dark brown sugar	1 teaspoon baking powder
1/3 cup butter	Pinch salt
1 egg	1/2 teaspoon vanilla
3/4 cup flour	1/2 cup chopped nuts

Melt sugar and butter together and cool. Add unbeaten egg. Sift together and add flour, baking powder and salt. Add vanilla and nuts. Bake in 9 inch square buttered pan at 330° for 45 minutes. —Mrs. Robert L. Martin

CHOCOLATE DREAMS
Bottom layer

1/2 cup brown sugar	1 cup flour
1/2 cup butter	1 teaspoon vanilla

Mix and press into pan—bake 10 minutes at 350°.

Topping

2 eggs, well beaten	1 teaspoon baking powder
1 cup brown sugar	1 cup chopped nuts
1 teaspoon vanilla	1 6-ounce package chocolate chips
2 tablespoons flour	

Mix and pour over baked bottom layer. Bake for 25 minutes at 350°. **—Mrs. Flora Leslie**

FROSTED CHOCOLATE DROP COOKIES

1 1/2 cups sifted flour	1/2 cup shortening, melted
1/4 teaspoon salt	1 cup brown sugar
1 teaspoon baking powder	1 egg
2 ounces unsweetened chocolate, melted	1/2 cup milk
	1 teaspoon vanilla

Sift flour, salt and baking powder together. Melt chocolate and add to shortening. Add sugar, egg, milk and vanilla, then add sifted ingredients. Let stand for 10 minutes. Drop from teaspoon onto greased baking sheet. Nut meats may be added. Bake at 375° for 12 - 15 minutes.

Frosting

1/3 cup butter	2 1/2 cups confectioners sugar
1/4 cup water	1 teaspoon vanilla
1/2 cup cocoa	

Melt butter over low heat with water. Remove from heat. Stir in cocoa. Mix in sugar 1 cup at a time. Beat until smooth and add vanilla. Add a little water if too thick. —Mrs. David G. Booth

CINNAMON DROPS

1 cup soft butter	1 teaspoon salt
2 cups brown sugar	1 teaspoon nutmeg
2 eggs	1 teaspoon cinnamon
1/2 cup cold strong coffee	1 cup raisins
4 cups flour	1/2 cup chopped nuts
1 teaspoon soda	

Mix and bake for 10 minutes at 400°.

—Mrs. Flora Leslie

COCONUT TARTS FOR TEA

3 cups all purpose flour	1 1/2 teaspoons salt
2/3 cup lard	1/4 cup cold water
1/3 cup butter	

Mix like pie crust and roll out dough; cut with fluted edged cutter to fit your muffin pans. Put 1 scant teaspoon of jelly in each cup. Then fill with the following mixture.

Filling

3 eggs, well beaten	1 1/2 tablespoons vanilla
1 1/2 cups sugar	2 tablespoons melted butter
1 1/2 cups chopped coconut	

Mix all ingredients together. Put 1 tablespoon of mixture in each tart shell and bake for 30 minutes at 375°.

—Mrs. Flora Leslie

COCONUT SQUARES
No. 1 Mixture

3/4 cup butter	1/2 cup brown sugar
1 cup all purpose flour	1 teaspoon lemon juice

Mix all together until it forms a paste. Pat into oblong 8 x 10 inch pan and bake for 15 minutes at 350°.

No. 2 Mixture

2 cups brown sugar	1 cup walnuts, cut fine or broken
2 whole eggs	1 can moist coconut
3 tablespoons all purpose flour	1 pinch salt
1/4 teaspoon baking powder	1 teaspoon vanilla

Mix in order given. Put on top of No. 1 mixture and bake for 20 minutes at 350°. Cut in squares.

—Mrs. David Emerman

HOLLY COOKIES
(For children to make)

38 large marshmallows	1 teaspoon vanilla
½ pound butter	5½ cups corn flakes
1½ teaspoons green food coloring (liquid)	Red cinnamon candies

Combine first four ingredients, melt over low heat, stirring until marshmallows are completely melted. Pour mixture over corn flakes. Stir gently until flakes are coated. Spoon onto plate, using a teaspoon, and shaping each mound into a generally round shape. Add three or four red cinnamon berries to each wreath. Let stand 24 hours.

—Mrs. Carlton A. Rasmussen

LEMON SOURS

⅔ cup flour	⅛ teaspoon baking powder
⅓ cup shortening	½ teaspoon vanilla
2 eggs	1 teaspoon lemon rind
1 cup brown sugar	2 tablespoons lemon juice
¾ cup coconut	1 cup confectioners sugar
½ cup nuts	

Sift flour. Cut in shortening to fine crumb stage. Pat into 8 x 8 inch pan and bake at 350° for 10 minutes. Beat eggs, add brown sugar, coconut, nuts, baking powder and vanilla. Spread over baked layer, return to oven and bake 20 minutes. Mix lemon rind, juice and confectioners sugar. Spread on top as soon as pan is removed from oven. Cool and cut into squares. Yield: about 2 dozen.

—Mrs. John P. Denio

MARSHMALLOW NUT ROLL

2 squares unsweetened chocolate, melted	1 teaspoon vanilla
	¾ cup chopped walnuts
1 cup confectioners sugar	2 cups miniature marshmallows
1 beaten egg	¾ cup coconut

Combine chocolate, sugar, egg and vanilla. Add walnuts and marshmallows. Spread coconut on sheet of wax paper. Spoon mixture onto coconut. Form roll. Chill and slice.

—Mrs. David G. Booth

PARTY PECAN COOKIES

1 egg white, well beaten
1 cup brown sugar
Dash of salt
1 teaspoon vanilla
2 cups whole, shelled pecans

Set oven at 450°. Add sugar to beaten egg white. Add salt and vanilla and blend well. Add nuts and mix until coated. Drop by teaspoonfuls on greased cookie sheet. Place in hot oven and turn off heat. Leave for 12 minutes.

—Mrs. Richard Thomas

CHOCOLATE RICE CRISPY BAR

1/2 pound marshmallows. Melt and mix in:
1/2 cup melted butter, then add
3 cups rice crispies
1 teaspoon vanilla

Mix and press lightly into buttered 9 x 9 inch pan. When cool cover with:

2 chocolate squares, melted
2 cups confectioners sugar
1 teaspoon vanilla
3 tablespoons hot water
2 tablespoons melted butter

—Mrs. Flora Leslie

SOUR CREAM COOKIES

1 cup butter
1 1/2 cups sugar
1 cup sour cream
3 eggs
4 cups flour
1 teaspoon soda
1 teaspoon baking powder
2 teaspoons lemon extract
2 teaspoons vanilla extract
1/4 teaspoon nutmeg

Cream sugar and butter. Add eggs and extracts. Add flour and dry ingredients. Add sour cream. Bake for 10 minutes at 400° until light colored. A teaspoon of jelly may be added on top, in the center.

—Mrs. Flora Leslie

TEA CAKES
(Nice to have on hand—the children love them)

3 cups flour
4 teaspoons baking powder
1/4 teaspoon salt
1 cup sugar
Rub in 1 cup butter
1 cup raisins
2 eggs, well beaten
1/2 cup milk
1 teaspoon vanilla

Mix and drop from spoon. Sprinkle with sugar. Bake for 10 minutes at 400°.

—Mrs. Flora Leslie

TOFFEE BARS

1 cup butter	2 cups flour
1 cup brown sugar	1/2 teaspoon salt
1 beaten egg yolk	1/2 pound milk chocolate bar
1 teaspoon vanilla	Walnuts, grated

Mix butter and sugar together. Add egg yolk, vanilla, flour and salt. Pat on pan or cookie sheet, approximately 11" x 15". Bake for 12 - 15 minutes at 350°.

Melt chocolate bar over hot water (not boiling). Spread over baked mixture. Top with grated walnuts. Cut in bars.

—Mrs. Louis A. Beer

UNBAKED COOKIES

2 cups sugar	1/2 cup peanut butter
1/2 cup milk	1 teaspoon vanilla
3 tablespoons cocoa	3 cups oatmeal
1 cup butter	1/2 cup nuts

Mix sugar, milk, cocoa and butter in saucepan. Bring to rolling boil for one minute; remove from heat and add peanut butter and vanilla. Mix until peanut butter is melted. Add oatmeal and nuts. Drop by teaspoonfuls onto wax paper to cool. A cookie much loved by children and easy enough for them to make themselves.

—Mrs. Donald S. Mann

CHEWY NOELS

2 tablespoons butter	1/8 teaspoon baking soda
1 cup brown sugar	1 cup chopped nuts
2 eggs	1 teaspoon vanilla
5 tablespoons flour	Confectioners sugar

Melt butter in an 8 x 8 inch pan. Combine sugar, eggs, flour, soda, nuts and vanilla and pour into pan. Bake for 20 minutes at 350°. Let cool a few minutes and invert on wax paper. Sift confectioners sugar over top. Cut into squares.

—Mrs. Carleton P. McLain, Jr.

BAKED APPLE PUDDING WITH RUM SAUCE

1 cup sifted flour	1/4 cup butter
1 teaspoon soda	1 cup sugar
1 teaspoon cinnamon	1 egg, unbeaten
3/4 teaspoon nutmeg	2 washed unpared large apples
1/4 teaspoon salt	

Sift together the first five ingredients. Mix butter with sugar and egg until fluffy. Grate apples medium fine, measure 2 cups, add to egg mixture. Blend in flour until just mixed. Pour in 8 x 8 x 2 inch pan. Bake at 400° for 25 - 35 minutes. Serve warm with rum sauce. Serves 8.

Rum sauce

1/2 cup butter	Dash nutmeg
1 cup sugar	1 teaspoon vanilla
1/2 cup light cream	2 - 3 tablespoons dark rum

Early in day in double boiler mix butter, sugar and cream. Cook, stirring 10 - 15 minutes until slightly thickened. Refrigerate. Fifteen minutes before serving add nutmeg, vanilla and rum. Reheat. Makes 1 1/2 cups. —**Mrs. W. Kent Barclay**

APPLE DUMPLINGS

8 cooking apples, pared and cored

Put each in center of square of pie crust. Fill center of apples with:

1 cup sugar	1 tablespoon cinnamon

Fold corners to center and pinch edges together. Make a syrup of:

2 cups sugar	1 package strawberry flavored
2 cups water	gelatin

Cook until syrupy. Pour over dumplings. Bake for 1 hour at 350° until apples are soft and pastry nice and brown. Serve warm. Serves 8. —**Mrs. Flora Leslie**

APPLE SAUCE CAKE
(Ice Box)

Put layer of cake broken up in bottom of pan. Thin layer of apple sauce well flavored with cinnamon and sugar. Another layer of broken cake. Another layer of applesauce. Whip 1 pint of whipping cream and spread over cake. Put in refrigerator over night. Serves 8 to 10. —**Mrs. Flora Leslie**

BAKED APPLE PUDDING
(German Apfelauflauf)

5 cups apples, peeled and sliced	2 cups milk
Sugar, cinnamon, butter	2 - 3 eggs
3 tablespoons corn starch	2 tablespoons raisins
4 tablespoon sugar	2 tablespoons almonds or nuts
1 teaspoon vanilla	

Heat oven to 400°. Put apples into 1½ quart baking dish. Sprinkle with sugar and cinnamon and dot with butter or margarine. Cover and place in oven. Simmer until soft.

In the meantime mix cornstarch, sugar, vanilla, eggs, milk and raisins. Pour over baked apples and sprinkle with almonds or nuts. Reduce heat to 350° and bake uncovered for about 50 minutes or until done. Serve hot or cold. —Mrs. Karl F. Koerner

UPSIDE-DOWN APPLE PIE

Make plain pastry for 9 inch double-crust pie.

2 tablespoons melted butter	½ cup granulated sugar
½ cup walnut halves	2 tablespoons flour
⅓ cup firmly packed light brown sugar	½ teaspoon cinnamon
	¼ teaspoon nutmeg
3 cups sliced tart apples	¼ teaspoon salt

Pour butter over the bottom of a 9 inch pan. Place walnuts flat side up in pan. Sprinkle with brown sugar. Lay bottom crust on top of this. Fill with apples, sugar, flour, cinnamon, nutmeg and salt mixed together. Cover with top crust. Prick and bake for 30 - 35 minutes or until pastry is nicely browned. Cool in pan about 5 minutes, then invert on a serving plate. Serve warm.
—Mrs. Donald S. Mann

BANANA CREAM PUDDING

¼ cup corn starch	3 beaten egg yolks
1 cup sugar	4 sliced bananas
1 teaspoon salt	Whipping cream
1 cup cold milk	Cherries
3 cups scalded milk	

Mix together first 3 ingredients, mix with cold milk and when smooth add to scalded milk. Cook until thickened, then add egg yolks mixed first with some of the warm pudding. Cook 10 minutes longer. Cool, add 4 sliced bananas. Top with whipped cream and a cherry. —**Mrs. Flora Leslie**

APPLE BETTY

4 cups chopped apples	2 cups apple juice
1 cup white sugar	1 cup melted butter
1 cup brown sugar	Cake or graham cracker crumbs
1 tablespoon cinnamon	

Mix altogether and put half of mixture in baking pan or 1½ quart casserole which has been lined with buttered crumbs. Add a layer of crumbs and then rest of apples. Cover with remainder of crumbs. Bake at 350° for 45 minutes. Serve with hard sauce.

Hard Sauce

2 cups confectioners sugar	1 teaspoon lemon extract
½ cup butter (room temperature)	1 teaspoon vanilla

Mix altogether. Serves 8 to 10.

—Mrs. Flora Leslie

APPLE STRUDEL
(Excellent for coffee or dessert)

2 cups all purpose flour	3 tablespoons sugar
3 teaspoons baking powder	4 tablespoons butter
½ teaspoon salt	¾ cup milk

Sift together dry ingredients. Cut in shortening and add milk to make soft dough. Turn out on floured board. Roll out ¼ inch thick. Brush with melted butter.

Cover with:	½ cup sugar
3 cups chopped apples	1 teaspoon cinnamon

Sprinkle apples with sugar and cinnamon. Roll like jelly roll into semicircle on greased baking sheet. Bake for 25 minutes at 425°.

While still warm pour white frosting over cakes.

2 cups confectioners sugar	1 teaspoon vanilla

Enough hot water to smooth. Pour over apple cake. Chopped nuts may be added. Serves 8 to 10.

—Mrs. Flora Leslie

BEST BIRTHDAY CAKE

1½ cups sugar
1½ cups flour
6 eggs
1⅓ teaspoons cream of tartar
½ cup cold water
¼ teaspoon salt
1 teaspoon vanilla
1 teaspoon lemon flavoring

Place egg whites in bowl and add salt. Beat until foamy and add ¾ teaspoon cream of tartar. Beat until stiff. Add slowly ½ cup sugar and the vanilla. Set aside.
Beat egg yolks until lemon color. Add lemon flavoring and remaining sugar. Add flour and remaining cream of tarter alternately with cold water. Fold in egg white mixture. Bake in angel food tube pan at 350° for 60 minutes.

—Mrs. David P. Williams

GLAZED BERRY PIE

2 boxes blueberries
1 cup sugar
3 tablespoons cornstarch
½ teaspoon butter
1 - 2 tablespoons lemon juice
Baked pie shell

Simmer 1 box blueberries in ¾ cup water for 3 minutes. To this add sugar and cornstarch. Stir and cook until thick and clear. Add butter and lemon juice. Pour this mixture over 1 box of fresh uncooked blueberries that have been placed in bottom of baked pie shell. Chill and top with whipped cream. Can be made with strawberries also.

—Mrs. Robert G. Wild

MY MOTHER'S BREAD PUDDING

3 slices white bread, generously spread with butter
3 eggs, slightly beaten
½ cup sugar
¼ teaspoon salt
½ teaspoon vanilla
1 pint milk

Place bread in buttered dish. Add sugar, milk, salt and vanilla to eggs. Strain and pour over bread in pudding dish. Bake about 45 minutes at 350° until firm and nicely browned. Serve with cream or hard sauce.

—Mrs. Clifford B. West

BUTTER HORNS

4 cakes yeast
1 cup milk, heated and cooled
1/2 cup sugar
1/2 cup melted butter
1 teaspoon salt
3 eggs
4 cups sifted flour

Dissolve broken up yeast in 1/3 cup milk for about 3 minutes. Do not stir. Beat eggs well and add butter, milk, salt and yeast. Beat well. Add flour gradually. Cover and put in ice box overnight. About 2 hours before serving, remove from ice box, roll bits of dough as for pie crust. Spread with melted butter and cut into pie shape pieces from center. Fill with desired filling and roll from wide end. Filling may be chopped nuts, cinnamon and sugar or jam or jelly. Place crescents on cookie sheet and let rise until double in bulk. Bake in moderate oven for 10 minutes.

—Mrs. Sherwin M. Birnkrant

DUTCH BUTTERCAKE SQUARES

1/4 pound butter
1 cup light brown sugar
1 egg
1 cup flour
Pinch of salt
1/8 teaspoon almond flavoring

Beat butter and sugar until fluffy. Add egg and mix well. Add flour, salt and almond flavoring. Bake in 8 inch pan about 20 minutes at 400°. Cut in squares.

—Mrs. Ben M. Snyder, III

FROZEN CHARLOTTE RUSSE

2 eggs
1/2 cup sugar
1 pint whipping cream
1/2 teaspoon vanilla or almond
    flavoring
Lady fingers
Strawberries

Add sugar to beaten egg yolks. Beat egg whites until stiff and fold into sugar and yolks. Fold in whipped cream. Add flavoring. Line the bottom and sides of a spring form pan with lady fingers packed closely together. Pour mixture into this and freeze. When ready to serve, carefully remove sides of pan and cover with strawberries, if you wish.

—Mrs. Max M. Fisher

LEMON CHEESE CAKE

1 cup boiling water
1 small package lemon flavored gelatin
Dissolve and cool but do not set.
2 8-ounce packages cream cheese

1 cup sugar
Beat together, add gelatin, then add
1 large can WHIPPED evaporated milk (chill before beating)
1 teapoon vanilla

Pour into graham cracker crumb shell. Sprinkle crumbs lightly on top. Do not bake. Chill. Makes one 9 x 14 inch or two 9 inch round cakes.

Graham Cracker Crumb Shell

2 tablespoons sugar
1/3 cup melted margarine

1 1/4 cups graham cracker crumbs

Press into pan to form shell.

—Mrs. David G. Booth

CHOCOLATE BOMBE

1 envelope unflavored gelatin
1 cup cold water
1 cup milk
1 1/4 cups sugar

2 tablespoons cocoa
1 teaspoon vanilla
2 cups heavy cream

Dissolve gelatin in cold water. Meanwhile stir and bring to boiling point milk, sugar and cocoa. Add gelatin to mixture. Cool. Add vanilla. Chill until thickening and about to set. Fold in whipped heavy cream and pour into mold. Freeze.

—Mrs. Richard A. Jones

COFFEE INTRIGUE

1 1/2 cups strong coffee
45 marshmallows
1 1/2 cups whipping cream

1 1/2 teaspoons vanilla
1 package lady fingers

Heat coffee and marshmallows in top of double boiler until marshmallows are dissolved. Set aside and allow mixture to begin to thicken, stirring occasionally. Beat cream until stiff, add vanilla and fold into coffee mixture and pour into serving bowl. Split lady fingers and push them down around the edge of the bowl into the mixture. Let stand overnight. When ready to serve, garnish with whipped cream and grated sweet chocolate.

—Mrs. Alfred C. Moore

CHOCOLATE ROLL

6 ounces dark sweet chocolate
3 tablespoons water
5 large eggs
¾ cup sugar

Confectioners sugar
Unsweetened chocolate
Whipping cream or strawberry
    preserves

Melt chocolate in water, then cool. Separate eggs. Beat yolks, adding sugar until almost white. Add chocolate to yolks. Butter freely one long cookie sheet with sides, then add waxpaper and butter again. Beat whites until stiff. Fold into mixture. Spread evenly in pan. Bake for 10 minutes at 350° then 5 minutes at 300°. Take out and lay a damp cloth not wrung too dry on the cake to keep a crust from forming. Let stand 5 minutes, then put it in the refrigerator from ½ to 1 hour. Take off cloth and put in oven for a few minutes to melt butter lining pan and then sprinkle with unsweetened chocolate. Cover with wax paper and turn over quickly. Strip paper off carefully. Spread whipped cream or strawberry preserves in strip down length of cake and flip over three times. Sprinkle a little confectioners sugar on top and allow to set one hour before serving.

—Mrs. Clifford B. West

DAIQUIRI PIE

4 egg yolks
1 cup sugar
½ teaspoon salt
½ cup lime juice
1 teaspoon grated lime rind
2 teaspoons unflavored gelatin
    soaked in ¼ cup cold water

4 egg whites
3 tablespoons light rum
½ pint whipping cream
Baked pie shell or graham cracker
    shell

Beat yolks, add ½ cup sugar, salt, lime juice and rind. Cook and stir in double boiler until thick. Add gelatin and stir until it dissolves. Cool. When beginning to set, beat egg whites until stiff with remaining sugar and fold them into mixture. Stir in rum. Chill until set and top with whipping cream.

—Mrs. G. Bretnell Williams

DATE ROLL

- 1 pound dates, pitted and chopped
- 1 pound miniature marshmallows
- 1 pound plus 6 graham crackers
- 1 pound chopped nutmeats (mild flavor nut)
- 1 pint heavy whipping cream
- Vanilla
- Sugar

Crumb graham crackers with a rolling pin. Combine all ingredients and mold into a roll. Roll in 6 more graham crackers which have been crumbled separately. Chill for 24 hours before serving. Cut into slices and serve with whipped cream, sweetened and flavored with vanilla.

Dessert for all ages and all seasons. Your teen-ager will love preparing this for family, your guests or her guests. Serves 6 to 12.

—Mrs. Spencer R. Hershey

FAVORITE FRUIT CAKE

- 5 large eggs
- 1/2 pound butter (no substitute)
- 1 cup white sugar
- 4 cups shelled pecans
- 3/4 pound candied cherries
- 1 pound candied pineapple (colored)
- 1/2 ounce pure vanilla
- 1/2 ounce pure lemon extract
- 1 3/4 cups regular flour
- 1/2 teaspoon baking powder

Chop nuts and fruit into medium-sized pieces. Cream butter and sugar until fluffy. Add well beaten eggs and blend until smooth. Mix fruit and nuts with part of flour to coat and separate pieces. Sift remaining flour and baking powder together. Fold into egg and butter mixture. Add flavorings, mix; add fruit and nuts, mixing well.

Pour into greased, waxed paper-lined tube pan. Place in cold oven then set at 250° and bake for 3 hours. Cool in pan on cake rack.

—Mrs. Harold D. Smart, Jr.

HEAVENLY DESSERT

1 10-ounce package vanilla wafers, crushed
½ pound butter
1 pound confectioners sugar
4 eggs
1 pint whipping cream
1 No. 2 can crushed pineapple

Mix butter and sugar. Add eggs one at a time beating well after each addition. Spread ½ of wafers in buttered 10 x 15 inch pan. Spread butter-sugar-egg mixture on top. Whip cream and add pineapple. Spread on top of No. 1 mixture and top with rest of crushed vanilla wafers. Let set several hours in refrigerator. Serves 20. —Mrs. Paul S. Gerhardt

GRASSHOPPER PIE

24 large marshmallows
⅓ cup milk
⅓ cup cream
1½ ounces green crème de menthe (3 tablespoons)
1½ ounces white crème de cacao (3 tablespoons)
½ pint whipping cream

Melt in double boiler: marshmallows, cream, milk and 2 liqueurs. Cool well. Fold in cream, whipped. Pour into chilled crust:

1⅓ cups crushed chocolate wafers
4 tablespoons melted butter

Refrigerate overnight. For an added treat, serve with a dab of vanilla ice cream on top, sprinkled with chocolate crumbs.
—Mrs. Charles L. Wilson, Jr.

HAZELNUSSTORTE
(Hazelnut Cake)

½ pound hazelnuts, ground fine
1 cup sugar
7 eggs
3 heaping tablespoons dried bread crumbs
1 teaspoon baking powder
½ teaspoon salt

Separate eggs and put one yolk aside for buttercream later. Beat the egg whites with half the sugar until extremely stiff (very important). Beat 6 egg yolks with rest of sugar until lemon color. Add nuts, bread crumbs, baking powder and salt. Fold in egg whites by hand but thoroughly until whites can no longer be seen in batter. Pour into greased springform pan. Bake at 350° - 375° for 40 minutes. Cool. Cut into 3 layers. Fill and cover with buttercream. (see page 70)

BUTTERCREME
(Buttercream)

- ¼ pound butter (room temperature)
- 2 ounces semi-sweet chocolate, melted
- 1 heaping tablespoon flour
- 2 tablespoons sugar
- Pinch of salt
- 1 cup milk (scant)
- ½ teaspoon vanilla
- Confectioners sugar

Mix flour, sugar, salt and milk in top of double boiler until smooth. Place over boiling water and cook until mixture thickens. Remove from fire and add 1 egg yolk stirring quickly. Cool. Cream butter in mixer. Add cooled mixture dropwise beating constantly. Add melted chocolate (cooled slightly). Beat thoroughly. Add vanilla and confectioners sugar to taste.

This torte must always be kept refrigerated. It keeps well and may be made 2 or 3 days before party. Or cake and frosting may be frozen and thawed just before serving.

—Mrs. Robert J. Schoenfeld

FUDGE BATTER PUDDING

- 2 tablespoons melted butter
- ½ cup sugar
- 1 teaspoon vanilla
- 1 cup sifted flour
- 3 tablespoons cocoa
- 1 teaspoon baking powder
- ½ teaspoon salt
- ½ cup milk
- ½ cup chopped nuts
- ½ cup sugar
- 3 tablespoons cocoa
- ¼ teaspoon salt
- 1½ cups boiling water

Mix first three ingredients. Sift next four ingredients and add to first mixture, alternately with milk. Mix well. Add nuts. Mix sugar, cocoa, salt and boiling water, and put into a 10 x 6 x 2 inch baking dish. Drop batter by spoonfuls on top. Bake 350° for 35 minutes. Serve warm or cold. —Mrs. Calvert Thomas

HAWAIIAN PUFFS

This is a pleasant variation of "some mores." Children love to prepare them outdoors over an open fire.

For each Hawaiian Puff use 2 graham crackers, one half slice of pineapple and 1 marshmallow. Toast the marshmallow slowly over the coals until it is light brown on the outside and soft all the way through. Make a sandwich using the 2 graham crackers for the outside and the pineapple and marshmallow for the filling. —Mrs. Janet M. Hawksley

HULDA'S MILE HIGH PIE

1 6-ounce box frozen strawberries
Pinch of salt
2 egg whites
1 cup sugar
1 cup whipping cream

Beat strawberries, salt, egg whites and sugar together in electric mixer for 15 minutes. Fold in whipped cream. Pile high in graham cracker crust and put in freezer for several hours.

Crust

15 graham crackers, crushed
Sugar
Butter
Mix together and bake 5 minutes

Makes two pies, using 8 inch pie plates. This is a wonderful recipe from a wonderful cook at Sunlight Ranch in Wyoming. Everyone looked forward to the days when Mile High Pie was on the menu. —Mrs. James H. Carmel

LEMONADE CAKE

1 package lemon cake mix
4 eggs
3/4 cup cooking oil
1 package lemon flavored gelatin, small size, dissolved in
3/4 cup of boiling water, cooled slightly
1 can thawed frozen lemonade
1/2 cup sugar

Mix first 4 ingredients, beat well, put in tube pan greased and lined with wax paper. Bake at 325° for an hour or until done. Turn out cake and immediately pour on lemonade mixed with sugar. —Mrs. Clifford B. West

SOFT MERINGUE

5 egg whites
1/2 teaspoon cream of tartar
1/4 teaspoon salt
1 1/2 cups sugar
1 teaspoon vanilla

Beat egg whites until foamy. Add cream of tartar and salt. Continue to beat until stiff. Gradually add sugar while beating. When sugar is all beaten in, continue to beat for 1 minute. Fold in vanilla. Turn into greased and floured 8 inch square pan. Place in oven 450°; then turn off heat and leave for 5 hours or overnight without opening oven. To serve cut into squares and top with vanilla ice cream and crushed fruit.

—Mrs. Richard Thomas

MOUSSE CHOCOLATE
For Top and Bottom

1/3 cup Brazil nuts, chopped	1/3 cup chocolate wafer cookies, made into crumbs

Filling

2 envelopes unflavored gelatin	1/2 teaspoon salt
1/2 cup cold water	1 cup milk
12 ounces semi-sweet chocolate morsels	6 eggs, separated
1 cup sugar	2 cups whipping cream

Soften gelatin in cold water. Add 1/2 cup sugar, salt and milk to chocolate. Cook until blended. Beat egg yolks and add to hot mixture slowly. Return to heat stirring constantly until thick. Remove from heat and add gelatin and stir well. Chill until thickened. Beat heavy cream. Beat egg whites stiff and add 1/2 cup sugar gradually while beating. Mix beaten yolks carefully into chocolate mixture, then add whipped cream and beaten egg whites very gently.

Line bottom and sides of large spring form pan with wax paper. Spread bottom with half the cookie and nut mixture. Add chocolate mixture, then top with rest of cookies and nuts. Chill. Serves about 12.

This is a very rich and impressive dessert. It can be decorated or topped according to one's own imagination.

—Mrs. Theodore Cooper

ORANGE SOUFFLE

4 egg whites	3 tablespoons orange marmalade
4 tablespoons sugar	1/4 teaspoon orange extract

Beat egg whites until stiff but not dry. Beat in sugar and fold in marmalade and orange extract. Cook for 1 hour in covered buttered double boiler. Turn out on serving dish and serve with sauce.

Sauce

2 eggs	2/3 teaspoon vanilla
1/2 - 1 cup confectioners sugar	Few grains salt

Beat egg whites until stiff and beat in half the sugar. Without washing beater, beat yolks until thick, adding remaining sugar gradually. Combine and flavor with salt and vanilla. This sauce separates if allowed to stand too long before serving. If this happens, merely stir again and serve. —Mrs. Richard F. Jones

FRESH PEACH CRISP

8 ripe peaches
3/4 cup packed brown sugar
1/2 cup sifted flour
1/8 teaspoon nutmeg
1/4 cup butter

Arrange peaches in bottom of shallow baking dish. Blend sugar, flour, nutmeg and butter with fingers to the consistency of fine crumbs. Sprinkle crumb mixture over peaches. Bake at 375° for about 25 minutes. Serve warm with ice cream or sauce.

Sauce

1/2 cup butter
Few grains salt
1 very ripe peach, mashed
2 tablespoons brandy (optional)
1 1/2 cups sifted confectioners sugar
Mix together.

—Mrs. A. William Reynolds, II

FRESH FRUIT SHERBET
(Delicious served as dessert or with roast beef dinner)

1 1/2 cups water
2 cups sugar
3 lemons
4 oranges
3 bananas

Make simple syrup of sugar and water and cook about five minutes. Squeeze lemons and oranges retaining much of pulp. Mash bananas. Mix fruits with cooled syrup and freeze. When ice begins to get mushy remove from freezing trays and stir well. Return to freezing compartment and freeze for 4 hours or more. Makes two ice trays full of sherbet.

—Mrs. Richard K. Scales

POPPY SEED CAKE

Beat together:
    1 cup butter
    1 1/4 cups sugar
    4 egg yolks

Add:
    1/2 pint sour cream
    1 teaspoon soda

Sift and mix in:
    2 cups flour
    3 teaspoons vanilla
    2 ounces dry poppy seed

Finally fold in:
    4 beaten egg whites

Bake at 350° in 10 inch tube pan for 50 - 60 minutes.

—Mrs. C. B. Sung

PECAN PIE
Flaky Pastry

Sift together:
2 cups flour
1 teaspoon salt
⅔ cup lard
6 tablespoons ice water

Mix ½ of shortening into flour until the size of a pea. Then mix in rest of shortening. Sprinkle ice water over flour. Mix quickly. Divide dough into 2 parts. Pat each half into a rounded cake. Roll out thin. Makes 1 double crust or 2 bottom crusts.

Filling

½ cup sugar
1 cup dark corn syrup
3 eggs
4 tablespoons butter, melted
1 teaspoon vanilla
1 cup broken pecan meats

Cook sugar and syrup until it thickens slightly. Beat eggs well. Add hot syrup slowly to eggs while stirring. Add melted butter, vanilla and nuts. Pour into uncooked pie shell and bake at 450° for 10 minutes. Reduce heat to 300° and bake for 35 minutes longer.
—Mrs. Calvert Thomas

QUICK DESSERT

1 can prepared pie cherries
½ box white cake mix
Butter
Nuts

Spread cherries in an 8 inch square pan. Cover with white cake mix. Slice butter very thin and cover mixture. Sprinkle nuts over top. Bake at 375° almost 1 hour until brown and crunchy on top.
—Mrs. Calvert Thomas

SCOTCH SCONES

2 cups all purpose flour
3 teaspoons baking powder
1 teaspoon salt
2 tablespoons sugar
4 tablespoons butter
2 eggs
½ cup milk
½ cup currants (optional)

Sift flour, baking powder and salt together. Cut in shortening; add currants. Beat 1 whole egg and 1 yolk, reserving 1 white for the tops. Add milk to beaten eggs. Add to dry ingredients. Stir only until dough holds together. Turn out on lightly floured board and knead gently. Cut into pie shaped pieces. Brush top with white of egg. Sprinkle with sugar. Bake for 12 - 15 minutes at 425°.
—Mrs. Flora Leslie

SOUR CREAM CHEESE CAKE

Filling

1½ pounds cream cheese
4 eggs, well beaten
1 cup sugar
1 teaspoon vanilla

Topping

½ pint thick sour cream
2 tablespoons sugar
½ teaspoon vanilla

Crust

3 cups graham cracker crumbs
¼ cup melted butter

Line a well greased spring form pan with a mixture of graham cracker crumbs and melted butter. Beat cream cheese in mixer until smooth. Add eggs and sugar. Beat mixture until creamy and add vanilla. Pour into pan and bake at 375° for 25 minutes. Remove from oven and allow to cool for 10 minutes. Increase heat to 475° and with spoon, carefully cover top of cake with sour cream, sugar and vanilla. Bake 5 minutes longer. Chill 12 - 24 hours. Use fresh or frozen berries on top.

—Mrs. Martin J. Kabcenell

SOUR CREAM COFFEE CAKE

1½ sticks margarine
1 cup sugar
2 eggs
2 cups flour
2 teaspoons baking powder
1 teaspoon soda
⅛ teaspoon salt
1 cup sour cream
1 teaspoon vanilla

Topping

1 cup brown sugar
1 teaspoon cinnamon
½ cup nuts

Cream together margarine, sugar and eggs. Sift flour, baking powder, soda and salt. Add sifted dry ingredients alternately with sour cream to creamed mixture. Add vanilla and pour batter into greased 9 or 10 inch tube pan. Pour ½ topping over batter and marble with knife. Sprinkle on remainder of topping. Bake at 350° for 40 - 50 minutes. Leave in pan to cool for at least two hours.

—Mrs. Richard Thomas

HOT MILK SPONGE CAKE

1 cup sifted cake flour
1 teaspoon baking powder
1/4 teaspoon salt
3 eggs, room temperature
1 cup sugar
2 teaspoons lemon juice
6 tablespoons hot milk

Sift flour 3 times after measuring with baking powder and salt. Beat eggs until thick, about 5 minutes, add sugar gradually beating constantly. Add lemon juice. Fold in flour. Add hot milk and stir quickly until blended. Turn at once into ungreased 9 inch tube pan and bake for 35 minutes at 350°. Invert pan for 1 hour when done. May be used for short cake.

—Mrs. David G. Booth

STRAWBERRY BAVARIAN

1 package vanilla pudding mix
2 cups milk
1 package strawberry flavored gelatin
1 cup hot water
1/2 cup cold water
Lady finger halves
Whipping cream

Prepare vanilla pudding with milk as directed on package. Chill. Dissolve strawberry gelatin in hot water. Add cold water. Chill until slightly thickened. Set bowl in ice and water and whip gelatin until fluffy. Add chilled pudding gradually. Beat after each addition. Spoon into large serving bowl lined with ladyfinger halves. Chill. Garnish with whipped cream. Serves 8 to 10.

—Mrs. William D. Seibert

STRAWBERRY PIE

Baked pie shell
1 1/2 quarts strawberries, fresh
1 cup sugar
3 tablespoons cornstarch
1 cup heavy cream
Vanilla

In baked pie shell arrange nicest berries, large end down. Mash rest of berries and stir into them the cornstarch and sugar which have been well mixed. Cook, stirring constantly, until thick. Set over hot water and continue to cook ten minutes. Mixture should be quite stiff. Cool and pour into pie shell over berries. Place in refrigerator and let the pie get very cold. When ready to serve, top with cream which has been whipped and flavored with vanilla and a little sugar.

—Mrs. Sherwin M. Birnkrant

SUNSHINE CAKE

⅓ teaspoon salt
¾ teaspoon cream of tartar
1½ cups sugar
1½ cups cake flour
11 large whites of eggs
8 yolks of eggs
1 teaspoon lemon extract
1 teaspoon lemon juice
1 rind of lemon

Sift flour once and measure. Sift sugar through onto wax paper. Remeasure half of sugar and sift together with flour 6 times. Beat egg whites with salt until foamy. Sprinkle in cream of tartar. Beat in ¾ cup of sugar. Beat egg yolks on number 8 until thick (about 15 minutes). Add rind of lemon, lemon juice and lemon extract to yolks. Fold in egg yolk mixture to whites. Take sifted flour mixture and add slowly to liquid mixture. Pour into large round tube pan. Bake for 65 minutes (30 minutes at 300° and 35 minutes at 325°).
—Mrs. A. Alfred Taubman

TORTE VIENNESE

6 eggs, room temperature
⅞ cup sugar
6 ounces ground walnuts, almonds or hazelnuts

Beat eggs until white and fluffy. Add sugar and beat again. Add walnuts. Pour into buttered and floured spring form pan. Bake at 350° about 45 minutes. Cake falls some.

Frosting

1 pint whipping cream
4 ounces semi-sweet chocolate bits

Bring cream unwhipped to boil. Add chocolate bits and melt. Refrigerate until very cold. Then whip cream and chocolate and spread on torte just before serving. The unfrosted cake may be frozen weeks ahead.   —Mrs. Philip E. Lachman

WEARY WILLIE CAKE

1 cup bread flour
1 cup sugar
1 teaspoon baking powder
¼ teaspoon salt
1 teaspoon vanilla
1 egg in 1 cup—fill cup with milk
2 squares chocolate, melted in
1 teaspoon butter

Stir all ingredients together. Bake in 8 inch greased pan at 350° until done. Test after about one half hour.
It is pretty simple even for a child to bake.
—Mrs. Terence E. Adderley

ADDITIONAL RECIPES
FROM
MRS. FLORA LESLIE

APPLE SALAD

2 cups unpeeled apples, chopped
1 cup celery, chopped
½ cup mayonnaise
3 tablespoons sugar
1 tablespoon lemon juice
¼ teaspoon salt

Mix all ingredients together and serve on lettuce leaf. Serves 6.

—Mrs. Flora Leslie

GERMAN NOODLES

1 pound medium size noodles (cooked and drained)
1 can cream of celery soup
1 can cream of mushroom soup
4 eggs, well beaten
½ pound sharp Cheddar cheese, grated
1 teaspoon salt
1 teaspoon paprika
½ teaspoon pepper

Cook noodles, rinse and drain. Add eggs to celery and mushroom soup. Stir in grated cheese, salt, paprika and pepper. Mix with noodles and put into greased casserole. Save a little cheese to sprinkle on top. Bake at 350° for 40 minutes. Serves 6.

—Mrs. Flora Leslie

BEEF POT PIE

2 pounds ground beef or round steak
2 tablespoons oil or margarine
3 large potatoes, cubed
3 large carrots, cubed
1 large onion, chopped
1 quart water
2 tablespoons Worcestershire sauce
2 teaspoons salt
1 teaspoon pepper
2 tablespoons Kitchen bouquet
¼ cup flour

Sauté ground beef in oil. Cook onion, potatoes and carrots in water until tender. Reserve liquid. Add cooked vegetables, Worcestershire sauce, salt, pepper and Kitchen bouquet to meat. Thicken with flour and reserved liquid. Put into large greased casserole and cover with biscuits.

Biscuits

2 cups flour
1 tablespoon baking powder
1 teaspoon salt
¼ cup lard
¼ cup butter
1 egg
⅔ cup milk

Mix all ingredients together. Turn out on lightly floured surface. Pat or roll ½ inch thick; cut with round cutter. Put on top of meat mixture. Bake at 425° for 10 minutes, then 350° for 20 minutes. Serves 8 to 10.

—Mrs. Flora Leslie

BAKED FISH
(Children's favorite fish)

10 4-ounce portions of uncooked, breaded fish (Cod or Haddock-no bones)

2 cups melted butter or margarine

Place fish on well greased pan. Pour melted butter over fish. Bake at 400° for 20-25 minutes or until golden brown. It is simple but good. Serves 8 to 10.

—Mrs. Flora Leslie

BARBECUED BEEF SANDWICHES

2 pounds ground beef
2 tablespoons oil or margarine
2 cups celery, chopped
2 cups onions, chopped
2 cups water
2 green peppers, chopped fine

1/2 cup tomato catsup
1 small can tomato sauce
2 teaspoons salt
1 teaspoon pepper
1 tablespoon sugar
2 tablespoons Worcestershire sauce

Sauté ground beef in oil. Cook celery, onions and green peppers in water until tender and add to ground beef. Add catsup, tomato sauce, salt, pepper, sugar and Worcestershire sauce. Simmer for 1 hour. Serve on hamburger buns. Serves 16.

—Mrs. Flora Leslie

ALMOND FORK COOKIES

2/3 cup butter
1 cup sugar
1 large egg
2 cups flour
1 teaspoon cream of tartar

1 teaspoon soda
1/4 teaspoon salt
1/4 teapoon nutmeg, freshly ground
1 teaspoon almond extract

Cream butter until soft. Add sugar, beat well. Add eggs and almond extract (no other liquid in recipe). Sift together flour, cream of tartar, soda, salt and nutmeg. Form dough into small balls, roll in sugar and press down on cookie sheet 3 times with fork. In place of almond extract an almond may be placed on each cookie. Bake at 400° for 8-10 minutes. Do not over bake. Makes 40-60 cookies.

—Mrs. Flora Leslie

STUFFED DATE COOKIES

1 pound pitted dates
4 ounces pecan halves
1/4 cup shortening
3/4 cup brown sugar, firmly packed
1 egg
1 1/4 cups sifted flour
1/2 teaspoon baking powder
1/2 teaspoon soda
1/4 teaspoon salt
1/2 cup sour cream

Stuff dates with pecans. Cream sugar and shortening. Add egg. Sift together flour, baking powder, soda and salt. Add sour cream and dry ingredients alternately to creamed mixture. Stir in dates. Drop on greased cookie sheet. Bake at 400° for 8-10 minutes. Makes 40 cookies. —Mrs. Flora Leslie

DELICIOUS COFFEE CAKE

1/2 cup butter
2 eggs
1 cup sugar
1 cup sour cream
2 cups flour
1/2 teaspoon soda
1 teaspoon baking powder
1/2 teaspoon salt
2 teaspoons vanilla

Cream together butter, eggs, sugar and vanilla. Beat well. Sift together flour, soda, baking powder and salt. Add sour cream and dry ingredients alternately to creamed mixture.

Topping

1/2 cup brown sugar
2 tablespoons flour
2 teaspoons cinnamon
1/2 cup chopped nuts

Mix all ingredients together.

Put one-half of topping into well greased angel food cake pan. Pour in one-half of the batter, then add remaining half of topping and remaining half of batter. Bake at 350° for 45 minutes. Turn upside-down on platter. Does not need icing. It is beautiful. —Mrs. Flora Leslie

RAISIN CAKE

3/4 cup butter
1 cup sugar
2 eggs
2 cups flour
1 cup raisins
2 tablespoons marmalade or jelly
1 teaspoon nutmeg
1 teaspoon cloves
1/4 teaspoon salt
1/2 teaspoon soda
1/2 cup sour cream

Cream butter. Add sugar and beat well. Add eggs and marmalade. Sift together flour, nutmeg, cloves, salt and soda. Add sour cream and dry ingredients alternately to creamed mixture. Stir in raisins. Pour into greased 9 inch square pan. Bake at 325° for 45-60 minutes or until lightly browned. Needs no frosting. Keeps well. —Mrs. Flora Leslie

INDEX

A

	Page
Almond Cookies, Oriental	53
Apple Betty	63
Apple Dumplings	61
Apple-Onion Soup	7
Apple Pie, Upside-Down	62
Apple Pudding, Baked	62
Apple Pudding, Baked with Rum Sauce	61
Apple Sauce Cake	61
Apple Strudel	63
Apricot-Date Bars	54
Aspic, Chicken Perfection	12
Avocado Dip	1

B

Baked Apple Pudding	62
Baked Apple Pudding with Rum Sauce	61
Baked Beans	32
Baked Chicken	37
Baked Chicken with Dressing	37
Baked Veal Chops with Curry Sauce	43
Banana Bread	48
Banana Cream Pudding	62
Bavarian, Strawberry	76
Bean Pot, Lima	33
Bean Salad	11
Bean Soup	7
Beans, Baked	32
Swiss	31
Beef Casserole	19
Beef Provencal	20
Beef Stroganoff (easy)	38
Berry Pie, Glazed	64
Best Birthday Cake	64
Biscuits, Cheese	1
Empire for Tea	53
Bigos	34
Black Cherry Salad	11
Blintz Pancakes	50
Bologna Buns	45
Bombe, Chocolate	66
Bouillon, Tomato	9
Bread, Banana	48
Irish Soda	48
Brown-Eyed Susan's	54
Brownies	53
Brownies, Butterscotch	55

	Page
Buffet Casserole	20
Buttercake Squares, Dutch	65
Butter Cookies	54
Butter Horns	65
Buttermilk Salad Dressing	17
Butterscotch Brownies	55
Burgers, Yorkshire	29
Burgundy Salad Dressing, Sparkling	17

C

Cake, Apple Sauce	61
Best Birthday	64
Cheese	66
Favorite Fruit	68
Hazelnusstorte	69
Hot Milk Sponge	76
Lemonade	71
Poppy Seed	73
Sour Cream Cheese	75
Sunshine	77
Weary Willie	77
Cakes, Tea	58
Carrot and Pineapple Salad, Jellied	11
Casserole, Beef	19
Buffet	20
Cauliflower and Tomato	31
Chicken Crab	21
Crab Meat	19
Eggplant	32
Fabulous Merger of Flavors	21
Frankfurter	22
Green Bean	32
Hamburger	19
Lima and Green Bean	31
Macaroni	23
Oyster	29
Pork Chop	24
Potato Chip	24
Wild Rice and Shellfish	28
Cat-Tail Pollen Pancakes	48
Cauliflower and Tomato Casserole	31
Celery Seed Salad Dressing	17
Charlotte Russe, Frozen	65
Cheese Biscuits	1
Cheese Cake, Lemon	66
Sour Cream	75

C—Continued

	Page
Cheese Pastry with Anchovies	1
Cheese Sandwiches, Toasted	46
Cherry Cream Ring	12
Cherry Salad, Black	11
Chewy Noels	59
Chicken, Baked	37
with dressing	37
Chicken Crab Casserole	21
Chicken Perfection Aspic	12
Chicken Salad, Hot	12
Chocolate Bombe	66
Chocolate Dreams	55
Chocolate Drop Cookies, Frosted	55
Chocolate Mousse	72
Chocolate Rice Crispy Bars	58
Chocolate Roll	67
Chocolate Sauce	9
Chop Suey	38
Chowder, Corn	7
Cinnamon Drops	56
Cinnamon Salad, Molded	13
Clam Dip	2
Coconut Squares	56
Coconut Tarts for Tea	56
Coffee Cake, Danish	47
Sour Cream	75
Coffee Intrigue	66
Coffee, Irish	5
Cole Slaw	11
Confetti Rice	25
Cookies, Butter	54
Brown-Eyed Susans	54
Cinnamon Drops	56
Frosted Chocolate Drop	55
Holly	57
Oriental Almond	53
Party Pecan	58
Sour Cream	58
Unbaked	59
Corn Chowder	7
Corn Pancakes	49
Crab Meat Casserole	19
Crab Meat Salad, Molded	13
Cranberry Salad, Frozen	14
Creole, Shrimp, a la	28
Creole, Spaghetti	25
Crumpets	47
Cucumber Salad, Jellied	14
Cucumbers in Cheese	33

D

	Page
Daiquiri Pie	67
Danish Coffee Cake	47
Date Bars, Apricot	54
Date Roll	68
Dip, Avocado	1
Clam	2
Washington, D. C.	2
Duck, French Roast with Wine Sauce	39
Duck, Venison, Elk	38
Dumplings, Apple	61
Dutch Buttercake Squares	65

E

Egg Nog Gentry	6
Eggplant Casserole	32
Eggplant, Italian	33
Empire Biscuits for Tea	53

F

Fabulous Merger of Flavors Casserole	21
Faucon Salad	14
Favorite Fruit Cake	68
Flank Steak	44
Foolproof Souffle	43
Frankfurter Casserole	22
French Pancakes	49
French Roast Duck with Wine Sauce	39
French Toast, Grandma's	50
Fresh Fruit Sherbet	73
Fresh Peach Crisp	73
Frosted Chocolate Drop Cookies	55
Frozen Cranberry Salad	14
Frozen Charlotte Russe	65
Fruit Cake, Favorite	68
Fudge Batter Pudding	70

G

Gelatin Salad	15
Glazed Berry Pie	64
Grandma's French Toast	50
Grasshopper Pie	69
Green Bean Casserole	32
Green Goddess Dressing	18
Green Grape Salad	15
Green Noodles al Pesto	24
Green Pea Soup	8
Grilled Tuna Fish	46

H

Ham, Chicken, Broccoli Mornay	23
Ham Loaf	39
Ham Loaf, Pineapple	39
Hamburger Casserole	19
Hamburgers	40
Hawaiian Curry	40
Hawaiian Puffs	70
Hazelnusstorte	69
Heavenly Dessert	69
Holly Cookies	57
Hot Chicken Salad	12
Hot Dogs, Sherwood	45
Hot Milk Sponge Cake	76
Hulda's Mile High Pie	71
Hungarian Pot Roast	41

I

Individual Turkey Pies	44
Italian Eggplant	33
Italian Shrimp Salad	16
Irish Coffee	5
Irish Soda Bread	48

J

Jellied Carrot and Pineapple Salad	11
Jellied Cucumber Salad	14

K

Koftas	40

L

Left-Over Delight With Stuffing	22
Lemon Cheese Cake	66
Lemon Sours	57
Lemonade Cake	71
Lima and Green Bean Casserole	31
Lima Bean Pot	33
Liver and Onions, Swiss	41
Liver Spread	2

M

Macaroni Casserole	23
Mahn-Go-Tah-See Mess	23
Marshmallow Nut Roll	57
Martha's Salad	13
Meat Balls, Sweet-Sour	42
Meat Sauce	10
Meat Spaghetti Sauce	10
Meringue, Soft	71
Milanesas	43
Miniature Mock Pizzas	3
Mint Sauce	9
Molded Cinnamon Salad	13
Molded Crab Meat Salad	13
Mousse, Chocolate	72
Mushroom Rolls for Cocktail Parties	3
Mushrooms in Sour Cream	34
Mustard Sauce	10
My Favorite Spaghetti with Hot Dogs	25
My Mother's Bread Pudding	64

N

Noodles al Pesto, Green	24
Nut Roll, Marshmallow	57

O

Open Face Sandwich	45
Orange Sherbet Punch	5
Orange Souffle	72
Oregano Spaghetti Sauce and Meat Balls	26
Oriental Almond Cookies	53
Oxtail Soup	8
Oyster Casserole	29

P

Pancakes, Blintz	50
Cat-Tail Pollen	48
Corn	49
French	49
Potato	49
Sour Cream	50
Pastry, Cheese with Anchovies	1
Party Pecan Cookies	58
Peach Crisp, Fresh	73
Pecan Cookies, Party	58
Pecan Pie	74
Pie, Daiquiri	67
Glazed Berry	64
Grasshopper	69
Hulda's Mile High	71
Pecan	74
Potato	34
Strawberry	76
Upside-Down Apple	62
Pies, Individual Turkey	44
Pineapple Ham Loaf	39

P—Continued

	Page
Pink Zip	4
Pizza	46
Pizzas, Miniature Mock	3
Poppy Seed Cake	73
Pork Chop Casserole	24
Pork, Sweet and Sour	42
Pot Roast, Hungarian	41
Potato Chip Casserole	24
Potato Pancakes	49
Potato Pie	34
Pudding, Baked Apple	62
Baked Apple with Rum Sauce	61
Banana Cream	62
Fudge Batter	70
My Mother's Bread	64
Yorkshire	51
Punch	5
Orange Sherbet	5
St. Dunstan's Christmas	6

Q

Quick Dessert	74

R

Rice, Confetti	25
Rice Crispy Bars, Chocolate	58
Rice, Spanish	26
Wild	34
Rolls, Mushroom for Cocktail Parties	3
Yeast	51
Romano Salad	16
Ruby Salad	14

S

Salad, Bean	11
Black Cherry	11
Cole Slaw	11
Faucon	14
Frozen Cranberry	14
Gelatin	15
Green Grape	15
Hot Chicken	12
Italian Shrimp	16
Jellied Carrott and Pineapple	11
Jellied Cucumber	14
Martha's	13
Molded Cinnamon	13
Molded Crab Meat	13
Romano	16
Ruby	14
Strawberry	16
Tossed Green	15
Salad Dressing, Buttermilk	17
Celery Seed	17
Green Goodess	18
Sparkling Burgundy	17
Salmon Loaf	41
Sandwich, Open Face	45
Sandwiches, Toasted Cheese	46
Sassafras Tea	6
Sauerkraut Mold	15
Sauce, Chocolate	9
Meat	10
Meat Spaghetti	10
Mint	9
Mustard	10
Oregano Spaghetti and Meat Balls	26
Scotch Scones	74
Sherbet, Fresh Fruit	73
Sherwood Hot Dogs	45
Shrimp a la Creole	28
Shrimp Salad, Italian	16
Shrimp Spread	3
Soda Bread, Irish	48
Soft Meringue	71
Soup, Apple-Onion	7
Bean	7
Green Pea	8
Oxtail	8
Tomato Wiener	8
U. S. Senate	9
Souffle, Foolproof	43
Orange	72
Spinach	35
Sour Cream Cheese Cake	75
Sour Cream Coffee Cake	75
Sour Cream Cookies	58
Sour Cream Pancakes	50
Spaghetti Creole	25
Spaghetti, My Favorite with Hot Dogs	25
Spaghetti Sauce, Meat	10
Spanish Rice	26
Spare-Rib Bites, Sweet-Sour	4
Sparkling Burgundy Salad Dressing	17

S—Continued

	Page
Spinach Souffle	35
Spread, Liver	2
Shrimp	3
Squash Rockefeller	35
St. Dunstan's Christmas Punch	6
Steak, Flank	44
Strawberry Bavarian	76
Strawberry Pie	76
Strawberry Salad	16
Strudel, Apple	63
Sweet and Sour Pork	42
Sweet-Sour Meat Balls	42
Sweet-Sour Spare-Rib Bites	4
Swiss Beans	31
Swiss Liver and Onions	41
Sukiyaki	27
Sunshine Cake	77

T

	Page
Tarragon Veal	44
Tarts, Coconut for Tea	56
Tea Cakes	58
Tea, Sassafras	6
Toasted Cheese Sandwiches	46
Toffee Bars	59
Tomato Bouillon	9
Tomato Wiener Soup	8
Tomatoes Stuffed with Grilled Mushrooms	36
Torte Viennese	77

	Page
Tossed Green Salad	15
Tropical Treat	27
Tuna Fish, Grilled	46
Turkey Pies, Individual	44
Turnip Fluff	35

U

	Page
Unbaked Cookies	59
Upside-Down Apple Pie	62
U. S. Senate Soup	9

V

	Page
Veal Chops, Baked with Curry Sauce	43
Veal, Tarragon	44
Viennese, Torte	77

W

	Page
Washington, D. C. Dip	2
Weary Willie Cake	77
Wild Rice	34
Wild Rice and Shellfish Casserole	28

Y

	Page
Yeast Rolls	51
Yorkshire Burgers	29
Yorkshire Pudding	51

ADDENDUM

RECIPES FROM MRS. FLORA LESLIE

A

	Page
Almond Fork Cookies	80
Apple Salad	79

B

	Page
Baked Fish	80
Barbecued Beef Sandwiches	80
Beef Pot Pie	79

D

	Page
Delicious Coffee Cake	81

G

	Page
German Noodles	79

R

	Page
Raisin Cake	81

S

	Page
Stuffed Date Cookies	81

Additional Recipes By Flora Leslie
Submitted by John Leslie and the Leslie Family

Ham Croquettes

3 tsp butter
¼ cup flour
1 cup whole milk
1/8 tsp. pepper

2 cups coarsely chopped ham
1 tsp. finely chopped onion
2 tsp. prepared mustard
dash of celery salt

Melt butter, blend in flour, add milk.
Cook and stir constantly until sauce is thick and smooth.
Remove from heat and add remaining ingredients.
Blend well, add salt if needed.
Chill mixture and shape into 8 – 9 balls.
Roll in 1 cup fine breadcrumbs, then shape into cones. Dip into mixture of 1 beaten egg and 1 tsp/ water, then roll in crumbs again.
Deep fry in hot oil (360 degrees F) for 2 – 3 minutes.
Serve with a creamy egg sauce.

- Mrs. Flora Leslie

Meatballs for a Cocktail Party

2 lbs ground steak
¼ cup chopped onions
1 egg
½ cup milk, salt and pepper
2 Ta Worchester sauce

Mix together and bake. Pour off grease.

Sauce
1 small jar currant jelly
½ cup tomato catsup
2 ta dry mustard

Mix together and heat just to melt jelly, tomato catsup and mustard. Serve ni a small serving bowl, or pour it over meat balls in a chafing dish.

- Mrs. Flora Leslie

Stuffed Mushrooms

12 – 16 large mushrooms
¼ lb. butter
1 tsp. Lawry's salt
1 pkg. lean pork sausage
3 large onions - chopped

Rinse mushrooms (dry thoroughly), remove and finely chop stems. In butter, sauté stems, onions, seasoning and sausage — remove skin if necessary, for approximately 5 minutes.
Spoon mixture into mushroom caps. Broil for about 8 minutes with stuffed side up. Add toothpick to each cap for serving.

- Mrs. Flora Leslie

Crab Canapés

2 cups whole milk
3 Tbs. cornstarch
3 Tbs. butter

Make a white sauce with the above ingredients.
Add 2 cans – 6 oz. drained crabmeat to sauce, also 1 Tbs. Worchester sauce, salt and pepper.
Take one large loaf of bread, white preferred.
Cut off the crust, then with a small cookie cutter or knife, cut into small squares. Cover with crab mixture, cover with shredded strong cheese. Bake until cheese is nice and brown — approximately 375 degrees (F) for 10 minutes.

- Mrs. Flora Leslie

Sugar Cookies - Delicious

1 cup butter
1 ½ cup sugar
3 eggs, 1 egg, 2 yolks
1 tsp. vanilla
(this makes about 8 dozen)

3 ½ cups sifted flour
2 tsp. cream of tarter
1 tsp. soda
½ tsp. salt

Cream butter, add sugar gradually, cream together until light and fluffy. Add eggs, one at a time, beating after each. Add vanilla, and sift dry ingredients. Chill at least 3 hours. Roll on a well – floured surface 1/8 to ¼" thick.
To hang on tree – make hole in top with a toothpick before baking. Bake on ungreased cookie sheet 375 degrees for about 6 – 8 minutes. Remove and cool on racks. Decorate when cool.

- Mrs. Flora Leslie

Spice Cookies

1 cup shortening (½ butter – ½ Crisco)
2 cups sugar
2 whole eggs
2 ½ cups flour
3 Tbl. sour milk

1 teaspoon cinnamon
1 tsp. cloves and mace
¼ tsp. salt
1 tsp. soda

Cream butter and sugar, add eggs, spices, then alternately flour and sour milk with soda dissolved.
Drop by teaspoons on buttered tins. Bake in a hot oven, 375 degrees (F) for 15 minutes.

- Mrs. Flora Leslie

Oatmeal Cookies

2 cups brown sugar
½ cup white sugar
1 cup rolled oats
½ cup flour
½ cup raisins

¼ cup butter
½ of ¼ cup of lard
1 egg
½ tsp. baking soda
pinch of salt.

Cream lard, butter and sugar together. Add flour, soda and salt sifted together, then rolled oats, and lastly the egg. This looks stiff and it should be.
Break up into small pieces and place on a greased pan quite far apart. Bake 15 – 20 minutes at 375 degrees (F), watching carefully so as not to burn.

- Mrs. Flora Leslie

English Plum Pudding

1 pound currants
12 ozs. Sultana raisins 1/2 pound glazed cherries 1 pound seeded raisins pound chopped suet
1 pound brown sugar
1 pound shredded mixed peel
1 pound peeled and chopped apples 1/2 pound bread crumbs
5 teaspoons baking powder
1/2 pound flour
1 cup butter
1 cup blanched and chopped almonds
2 orange rinds grated
2 lemon rinds grated
1 Tablespoon nutmeg
1 Tablespoon cinnamon
1 Tablespoon ginger
1 cup brandy or fruit juice
6 eggs
1/2 teaspoon mace
1/2 teaspoon soda

Mix and let stand over night. Put into greased bowls next morning and steam six hours. Makes four large puddings. Cover the puddings with greased paper (wax paper) and cloth before steaming.
Steam two hours before serving. Serve with hard sauce.

- **Mrs. Flora Leslie**

www.ingramcontent.com/pod-product-compliance
Lightning Source LLC
LaVergne TN
LVHW011713060526
838200LV00051B/2888